GUIDE TO

Proposal Writing

FOURTH EDITION

Jane C. Geever

Library of Congress Cataloging-in-Publication Data

Geever, Jane C.
   The Foundation Center's guide to proposal writing / Jane C.
Geever.— 4th ed.
         p. cm.
   Includes bibliographical references.
   ISBN 1-931923-92-2 (hardcover)
   1. Proposal writing for grants—United States—Handbooks, man-
uals, etc.   I. Title: Guide to proposal writing. II. Foundation Center.
III. Title.

HG177.5.U6G44 2004
   658.15'224—dc22

                                                        2004001070

Contents

Preface

For many years, grantseekers using Foundation Center libraries, our Web site, and print and electronic directories have been asking us for help beyond research into potential funders for their work. They need assistance in writing the proposal and advice on the proper way to submit it, given the widely differing policies and preferences among foundations and corporate grantmakers. To respond to this demand, in 1993 we commissioned Jane C. Geever and Patricia McNeill of the firm J. C. Geever, Inc., to write a guide for us, based on their many years of fundraising experience and knowledge of a great variety of grantmakers. Several editions followed, and the *Guide* as well as seminars we offer based on the advice herein have proven very popular with our audiences. This fourth edition includes responses to a new series of interview questions by 40 grantmakers and excerpts from actual proposals to illustrate the text.

We hope this guide to proposal writing proves useful to all of you who are seeking grants, and we would welcome your comments and reactions to it.

We wish to thank the following grantmakers who participated in the interviews for their time and the valuable insights they provided:

Joseph S. Dolan, Executive Director
The Achelis and Bodman
  Foundations
New York, NY

Karen L. Rosa, Vice President and
  Executive Director
Altman Foundation
New York, NY

Mary Beth Salerno, President
American Express Foundation
New York, NY

Mary L. Gregory, Executive
  Director
Bella Vista Foundation
San Francisco, CA

James V. DeNova, Senior Program
  Officer
Claude Worthington Benedum
  Foundation
Pittsburgh, PA

Laura H. Gilbertson, Director
Elizabeth B. Meers, Public
  Relations Committee Chair
The William Bingham Foundation
Rocky River, OH

David A. Odahowski, President
  and CEO
Edyth Bush Charitable Foundation
Winter Park, FL

Rebecca Martin, Director Grants
  Administration
The California Endowment
Woodland Hills, CA

Marci Lu, Program Officer
The Cleveland Foundation
Cleveland, OH

David K. Gibbs, Senior Program
  Officer
The Community Foundation for
  Greater Atlanta
Atlanta, GA

Ruby Lerner, Executive Director
Creative Capital Foundation
New York, NY

J. Andrew Lark, Co-Trustee
The Frances L. & Edwin L.
  Cummings Memorial Fund
New York, NY

Ruth Shack, President
Dade Community Foundation
Miami, FL

A. Thomas Hildebrandt, Director
The Davenport-Hatch Foundation,
  Inc.
Rochester, NY

David Grant, Executive Director
Cynthia Evans, Comptroller
Geraldine R. Dodge Foundation
Morristown, NJ

David Palenchar, Senior Vice
  President, Operations
El Pomar Foundation
Colorado Springs, CO

Jeffrey H. Schwartz, Senior
  Director, National Initiatives
Fannie Mae Foundation
Washington, DC

Peter F. Bird, CEO
Frist Foundation
Nashville, TN

Richard K. Jung, Senior Program
   Officer
Gill Foundation
Denver, CO

William V. Engel, Executive
   Director and Trustee
E.J. Grassmann Trust
Warren, NJ

Ilene Mack, Senior Program Officer
William Randolph Hearst
   Foundation
New York, NY

David O. Egner, President
Hudson-Webber Foundation
Detroit, MI

Elizabeth B. Smith, Executive
   Director
The Hyams Foundation, Inc.
Boston, MA

Hunter W. Corbin, President
The Hyde and Watson Foundation
Chatham, NJ

Robert Crane, President
JEHT Foundation
New York, NY

Eugene R. Wilson
Senior Vice President, Strategic
   Programs and Planning
Ewing Marion Kauffman
   Foundation
Kansas City, MO

Roxanne Ford, Program Director
W.M. Keck Foundation
Los Angeles, CA

Penelope L. McPhee, Vice President
   and Chief Program Officer
John S. and James L. Knight
   Foundation
Miami, FL

John E. Marshall III, President and
   CEO
The Kresge Foundation
Troy, MI

Christine Park, President
Lucent Technologies Foundation
Murray Hill, NJ

Elspeth Revere, Director, General
   Program
John D. and Catherine T.
   MacArthur Foundation
Chicago, IL

Bruce H. Esterline, Vice President
   for Grants
The Meadows Foundation, Inc.
Dallas, TX

Hildy Simmons, Independent
   Philanthropic Adviser
Formerly of J.P. Morgan Private
   Bank
New York, NY

Elan Garonzik, Program Officer
Charles Stewart Mott Foundation
Flint, MI

Maria Mottola, Executive Director
New York Foundation
New York, NY

Nancy Wiltsek, Executive Director
Pottruck Family Foundation
San Francisco, CA

Larry Kressley, Executive Director
Public Welfare Foundation
Washington, DC

David Ford, Executive Director
Richard and Susan Smith Family
    Foundation
Chestnut Hill, MA

E. Belvin Williams, Executive
    Director
Turrell Fund
Montclair, NJ

P. Russell Hardin, Vice President
Robert W. Woodruff Foundation, Inc.
Atlanta, GA

We also wish to thank the following nonprofit organizations whose leaders graciously permitted us to use excerpts from their proposals to illustrate the text:

American Institute of Chemical
    Engineers
New York, NY
Scott J. Hamilton, Director of
    Planning, Development &
    Corporate Communications

Appalachian Citizens Law Center
Prestonburg, KY
Stephen A. Sanders, Director

Arts In Progress
Boston, MA
Robert F. Wooler, Executive
    Director

Booker T. Washington Learning
    Center
New York, NY
Rev. Leroy Ricksy, Executive
    Director

Canal Community Alliance
San Rafael, CA
Tom Wilson, Executive Director

Center for Family Representation
Brooklyn, NY
Susan Jacobs, Executive Director

Christ's Outreach for the Blind
Mt. Vernon, KY
Michael Gates, President

City Life/Vida Urbana
Jamaica Plain, MA
Juan E. Leyton, Executive Director

Cora Hartshorn Arboretum and
    Bird Sanctuary
Short Hills, NJ
Christie Adelman, President

East Side House Settlement
Bronx, NY
John A. Sanchez, Executive
    Director

Edgewood Center for Children and
    Families
San Francisco, CA
Nancy Rubin, Chief Executive
    Officer

Family Focus
Chicago, IL
Kevin Limbeck, Executive Director

Fieldstone Farm Therapeutic
Riding Center
Chagrin Falls, OH
Lynnette R. Stuart, Executive
Director

Good Shepherd Services
New York, NY
Sr. Paulette LoMonaco, Executive
Director

Groundwork
Brooklyn, NY
Richard R. Buery, Executive
Director

Habitat for Humanity of San
Antonio
San Antonio, TX
Dennis L. Bechhold, President &
CEO

Hathaway Brown School
Shaker Heights, OH
William Christ, Head of School

King Manor Museum
Jamaica, NY
Mary Anne Mrozinski, Executive
Director

Mount Saint Mary Academy
Watchung, NJ
Sister Lisa Gambacorto, RSM,
Directress

National Hemophilia Foundation
New York, NY
Cheryl Baun, Manager of
Foundation Relations

NPower NY
New York, NY
Barbara Chang, Executive Director

Ridgewood YMCA and the YWCA
of Bergen County
Ridgewood, NJ
Lewis S. Dickinson, Vice President,
Development

Sembrando Flores
Homestead, FL
Nancy Rivera, Executive Director

Teach For America • New Jersey
Newark, NJ
John C. White, Executive Director

Women Express/*Teen Voices*
Boston, MA
Jenny Amory, Executive Director

World Impact, Inc.
Newark, NJ
Dr. D. Fred Clark, Director

YMCA of Eastern Union County
Elizabeth, NJ
Dale Timmons Evanson, Director of
Development

From the Author

Proposal writing is essential to the fundraising process, but it can be intimidating for the novice. There is nothing worse than staring at a blank piece of paper or computer screen with the sinking feeling that so much is riding on the prose you must create. Yet, if you follow the step-by-step process described in this book, you can create a proposal with a minimum of anxiety.

Take the steps one at a time. You will be successful in writing exciting and compelling proposals, proposals that will capture the interest of foundations and corporations, proposals that will generate grant support for your nonprofit organization.

In preparing this book, I interviewed a cross section of foundation and corporate representatives to find out their current thoughts on what should go into a proposal. While this material reinforces the steps I describe for writing a proposal, it also presents some notable insights into how grantmakers do their work, the challenges facing funders today, and how they are responding. These insights are a distinguishing feature of this book: They show the reality of the fundraising process from the funder's side of the proposal.

The 40 funding representatives interviewed include a geographic mix of local and national grantmakers, as well as representatives of independent, corporate, and community foundations and grant-making public charities. Some of the funders represented have been in existence for many years. Others are fairly new. All are large enough to have at least one person on staff, and some employ many people.

While the grantmakers interviewed reflect a relatively broad spectrum, it is important to remember that there are more than 65,000 private foundations in the United States. The majority of these have no staff and in fact are so small that the few local grants they award each year can be handled by trustees, lawyers, or family members. Therefore, the comments made here do not necessarily apply to all funders, but they do provide an indication of how some of the larger funders operate and how they evaluate the proposals they receive.

A series of questions was designed for the interview sessions in order to elicit views not only on proposal writing but also on the entire funding process and particularly on the impact of the economy on this process. Interviews were conducted via the telephone, following a questionnaire format. Questions were posed as to desired proposal contents, layout, length, and presentation. Funders were asked how proposals captured and kept their attention, what the characteristics of a successful proposal are, and what red flags are raised when they read proposals. They were also asked to discuss follow-up strategies once an agency receives a grant and whether, and how, to resubmit a rejected proposal. They were asked to describe trends they perceived in the current funding climate.

Information and quotes gleaned from these interviews are used throughout the text. Chapter 13, "What the Funders Have to Say," reflects the substance of the interviews. Here, the reader will find specific questions asked of each grantmaking representative with some of their responses. The goal in presenting this information is distinctly not to help the reader learn about particular funders but rather to provide a more general sense of grantmakers' perspectives on proposal writing. The funders interviewed have spoken frankly.

They have all granted permission to the Foundation Center to use their quotes.

Acknowledgments

I would like to express appreciation to the staff of J. C. Geever, Inc., particularly to Cheryl Austin who helped prepare the manuscript, and to Judi Margolin, Margaret Morth, and Christine Innamorato of the Foundation Center who saw this guide through production.

Introduction

If you are reading this book, you probably have already decided that foundations should be part of your fundraising strategy. You should be aware that, together, foundations and corporations provide only 16.3 percent of private gift support to nonprofit institutions. Their support, however, can be extremely important in augmenting other forms of income, in permitting major new initiatives, or simply in promoting the mission of your agency.

Over the past decade the number of foundations has nearly doubled, while their assets and giving have roughly tripled. In 2001, foundations held combined assets of close to $470 billion. For 2002, their estimated giving totaled over $30 billion. Despite an extended economic downturn in the early years of the new century, the foundation community overall can be expected to maintain the gains recorded in the late 1990s.

Unfortunately, competition for these grant dollars has also increased. Many nonprofits were created to respond to new or heightened social needs during the 1990s. In the early 21st century some of these nonprofit organizations have fallen by the wayside or merged with other similar organizations. Cutbacks in government funding for nonprofit services and activities have meant that many groups that previously relied primarily on government funds are now turning to private sources to support their work. Meanwhile, private foundations have experienced significant reductions in their own assets due to stock market losses.

In comparison with the figures for foundation giving, according to the AAFRC Trust for Philanthropy, giving by living individuals was $183.7 billion in 2002, six times that of foundations. (Bequests totaled an additional $18.1 billion.) What you need to attract donors to your agency is a comprehensive fundraising strategy that includes a variety of sources and approaches. This book focuses on how to create proposals to win foundation and corporate support.

You will want to tell your story clearly, keeping the interests of those you are approaching in mind. You need to recognize the potential for partnership with those you are approaching.

The Proposal Is Part of a Process

The subject of this book is proposal writing. But the proposal does not stand alone. It must be part of a process of planning and of research on, outreach to, and cultivation of potential foundation and corporate donors.

This process is grounded in the conviction that a partnership should develop between the nonprofit and the donor. When you spend a great deal of your time seeking money, it is hard to remember that it can also be difficult to give money away. In fact, the dollars contributed by a foundation or corporation have no value until they are attached to solid programs in the nonprofit sector.

This truly *is* an ideal partnership. The nonprofits have the ideas and the capacity to solve problems, but no dollars with which to implement them. The foundations and corporations may have the financial resources but not necessarily the other resources needed to create programs. Bring the two together effectively, and the result is a dynamic collaboration. Frequently, the donor is transformed into a stakeholder in the grantee organization, becoming deeply interested and involved in what transpires.

"There is a partnership in philanthropy," says Roxanne Ford of the W.M. Keck Foundation. "We need the grantees. We are only an enabler of good work. The Foundation is grateful to the nonprofit organizations that work with us." Robert Crane of the JEHT Foundation adds: "We want to be user-friendly, and build honest relationships." And Jim Denova of the Claude Worthington Benedum Foundation suggests that grantmakers "... absolutely prefer to get involved as early as possible—doing concept work, helping shape an idea."

You need to follow a step-by-step process in the search for private dollars. Nancy Wiltsek of the Pottruck Family Foundation admonishes, "Abide by the process!" It takes time and persistence to succeed. After you have written a proposal, it could take a year or more to obtain the funds needed to carry it out. And even a perfectly written proposal submitted to the right prospect might be rejected for any number of reasons.

Raising funds is an investment in the future. Your aim should be to build a network of foundation and corporate funders, many of which give small gifts on a fairly steady basis, and a few of which give large, periodic grants. By doggedly pursuing the various steps of the process, each year you can retain most of your regular supporters and strike a balance with the comings and goings of larger donors. The distinctions between support for basic, ongoing operations and special projects are discussed elsewhere in this book. For now, keep in mind that corporate givers and small family foundations tend to be better prospects for annual support than the larger, national foundations.

The recommended process is not a formula to be rigidly adhered to. It is a suggested approach that can be adapted to fit the needs of any nonprofit and the peculiarities of each situation. Fundraising is an art, not a science. You must bring your own creativity to it and remain flexible.

An example might help. It is recommended that you attempt to speak with the potential funder prior to submitting your proposal. The purpose of your call is to test your hypothesis gleaned from your research about the potential match between your nonprofit organization and the funder. Board member assistance, if you are fortunate enough to have such contacts, ordinarily would not come into play until a much later stage. But what do you do if a board member indicates that his law partner is chairman of the board of a foundation you plan to approach? He offers to submit the proposal directly to his partner. You could refuse the offer and plod through the next steps, or you could be flexible in this instance, recognizing that your agency's likelihood of being funded by this foundation might have just risen dramatically. Don't be afraid to take the risk.

Recognizing the importance of the process to the success of your agency's quest for funds, let's take a look at each step.

Step One: Setting Funding Priorities

In the planning phase, you need to map out all of your agency's priorities, whether or not you will seek foundation or corporate grants for them. Ideally these priorities are determined in an annual planning session. The result of the meeting should be a solid consensus on the funding priorities of your organization for the coming year. Before seeking significant private sector support, you need to decide which of your organization's funding priorities will translate into good proposals. These plans or projects are then developed into funding proposals, and they form the basis of your foundation and corporate donor research.

Step Two: Drafting the Basic or "Master" Proposal

You should have at least a rough draft of your proposal in hand before you proceed, so that you can be really clear about what you'll be asking funders to support. In order to develop a "master" proposal, you will need to assemble detailed background information on the project, select the proposal writer, and write the actual components of the document, including the executive summary, statement of need, project description, budget, and organizational information.

Step Three: Packaging the Proposal

At this juncture you have laid the groundwork for your application. You have selected the projects that will further the goals of your organization. You have written the master proposal, usually a "special project" proposal, or a variation, such as one for a capital campaign or endowment fund.

Before you can actually put the document together and get it ready to go out the door, you will need to tailor your "master" proposal to the specific funder's priorities. When you have taken that step, you will need to add a cover letter and, where appropriate, an appendix, paying careful attention to the components of the package and how they are put together.

Step Four: Researching Potential Funders

You are now ready to identify those sources that are most likely to support your proposal. You will use various criteria for developing your list, including the funders' geographic focus and their demonstrated interest in the type of project for which you are seeking funds. This research process will enable you to prepare different finished proposal packages based on the guidelines of specific funders.

Step Five: Contacting and Cultivating Potential Funders

This step saves you unnecessary or untimely submissions. Taking the time to speak with a funder about your organization and your planned proposal submission sets the tone for a potentially supportive future relationship, *if* they show even a glimmer of interest in your project. This step includes judicious use of phone and/or e-mail communication, face-to-face meetings, board contacts, and written updates and progress reports. Each form of cultivation is extremely important and has its own place in the fundraising process. Your goal in undertaking this cultivation is to build a relationship with the potential donor and to communicate important information while your request is pending. Persistent cultivation keeps your agency's name in front of the foundation or corporation. By helping the funder learn more about your group and its programs, you make it easier for them to come to a positive response on your proposal—or, failing that, to work with you in the future.

Step Six: Responding to the Result

No matter what the decision from the foundation or corporate donor, you must assume responsibility for taking the next step. If the response is positive, good follow-up is critical to turning a mere grant into a true partnership.

Unfortunately, even after you have followed all of the steps in the process, statistically the odds are that you will learn via the mail or a phone call that your request was denied. Follow-up is important here, too, either to find out if you might try again at another time or with another proposal or to learn how to improve your chances of getting your proposal funded by others.

1

Getting Started: Establishing a Presence and Setting Funding Priorities

Every nonprofit organization needs to raise money. That is a given. Yet some nonprofits believe that their group must look special or be doing something unique before they are in a position to approach foundations and corporate grantmakers for financial support. This assumption is mistaken. If your organization is meeting a valid need, you are more than likely ready to seek foundation or corporate support.

But three elements should already be in place. First, your agency should have a written mission statement. Second, your organization should have completed the process of officially acquiring nonprofit status, or you need to have identified an appropriate fiscal agent to receive the funds on your behalf. Finally, you should have credible program or service achievements or plans in support of your mission.

Mission Statement

When your agency was created, the founders had a vision of what the organization would accomplish. The mission statement is the written summary of that vision. It is the global statement from which all of your nonprofit's programs and services flow. Such a statement enables you to convey the excitement of the purpose of your nonprofit, especially to a potential funder who has not previously heard of your work. Of course, for you to procure a grant, the foundation or corporation must agree that the needs being addressed are important ones.

Acquiring Nonprofit Status

The agency should be incorporated in the state in which you do business. In most states this means that you create bylaws and have a board of directors. It is easy to create a board by asking your close friends and family members to serve. A more effective board, though, will consist of individuals who care about the cause and are willing to work to help your organization achieve its goals. They will attend board meetings, using their best decision-making skills to build for success. They will actively serve on committees. They will support your agency financially and help to raise funds on its behalf. Potential funders will look for this kind of board involvement.

In the process of establishing your nonprofit agency, you will need to obtain a designation from the federal Internal Revenue Service that allows your organization to receive tax-deductible gifts. This designation is known as 501(c)(3) status. A lawyer normally handles this filing for you. Legal counsel can be expensive. However, some lawyers are willing to provide free help or assistance at minimal cost to organizations seeking 501(c)(3) status from the IRS.

Once your nonprofit has gone through the filing process, you can accept tax-deductible gifts. If you do not have 501(c)(3) status and are not planning to file for it in the near future, you can still raise funds. You will need to find another nonprofit with the appropriate IRS designation willing to act as a fiscal agent for grants received by your agency. How does this work? Primary contact will be between your organization and the funder. The second agency, however, agrees to be responsible for handling the funds and providing financial reports. The funder will require a formal written statement from the agency serving as fiscal agent. Usually the fiscal agent will charge your organization a fee for this service.

Credible Programs

Potential funders will want to know about programs already in operation. They will invest in your agency's future based on your past achievements. You will use the proposal to inform the funder of your accomplishments, which should also be demonstrable if an on-site visit occurs.

If your organization is brand new or the idea you are proposing is unproven, the course you plan to take must be clear and unambiguous. Your plan must be achievable and compelling. The expertise of those involved must be relevant. Factors such as these must take the place of a track record when one does not yet exist. Funders are often willing to take a risk on a new idea, but be certain that you can document the importance of the idea and the strength of the plan.

Like people, foundations have different levels of tolerance for risk. Some will invest in an unknown organization because the proposed project looks particularly innovative. Most, however, want assurance that their money is going to an agency with strong leaders who have proven themselves capable of implementing the project described in the proposal.

What really makes the difference to the potential funder is that your nonprofit organization has a sense of direction and is implementing, or has concrete plans to implement, programs that matter in our society. You have to be able to visualize exciting programs and to articulate them via your proposal. Once you've got these three elements in place, you're ready to raise money from foundations and corporations!

Setting Funding Priorities

Once your organization has established a presence, the first step of the proposal process is determining the priorities of your organization. Only after you do that can you select the right project or goals to turn into a proposal.

Your Priorities

There is one rule in this process: You must start with your organization's needs and then seek funders that will want to help with them. Don't start with a foundation's priorities and try to craft a project to fit them. Chasing the grant dollar makes little sense from the perspectives of fundraising, program design, or agency development.

When you develop a program tailored to suit a donor, you end up with a project that is critically flawed. First, in all likelihood the project will be funded only partially by the grant you receive. Your organization is faced with the dilemma of how to fund the rest of it. Further, it will likely be hard to manage the project as part of your total program without distorting your other activities. Scarce staff time and scarcer operating funds might have to be diverted from the priorities you have already established. At worst, the project might conflict with your mission statement.

Start with a Planning Session

A planning session is an excellent way to identify the priorities for which you will seek foundation grants and to obtain agencywide consensus on them. Key board members, volunteers, and critical staff, if your agency has staff, should come together for a several-hour discussion. Such a meeting will normally occur when the budget for the coming fiscal year is being developed. In any case, it cannot be undertaken until the overall plan and priorities for your organization are established.

The agenda for the planning session is simple. With your organization's needs and program directions clearly established, determine which programs, needs, or activities can be developed in proposal form for submission to potential funders.

Apply Fundability Criteria

Before moving ahead with the design of project proposals, test them against a few key criteria:

1. The money cannot be needed too quickly. It takes time for funders to make a decision about awarding a grant. If the foundation or corporate grantmaker does not

know your agency, a cultivation period will probably be necessary.

A new program can take several years to be fully funded, unless specific donors have already shown an interest in it. If your new program needs to begin immediately, foundation and corporate donors might not be logical sources to pursue. You should begin with other funding, from individuals, churches, or civic groups, from earned income, or from your own operating budget, or else you should delay the start-up until funding is secured from a foundation or corporate grantmaker.

A project that is already in operation and has received foundation and corporate support stands a better chance of attracting additional funders within a few months of application. Your track record will provide a new funder with an easy way to determine that your nonprofit can deliver results.

2. Specific projects tend to be of greater interest to most foundation and corporate funders than are general operating requests. This fundraising fact of life can be very frustrating for nonprofits that need dollars to keep their doors open and their basic programs and services intact. There is no doubt, though, that it is easier for the foundation or corporate funder to make a grant when the trustees will be able to see precisely where the money is going, and the success of their investment can be more readily assessed.

Keep in mind the concerns of the foundation and corporate funders about this question when you are considering how to develop your proposals for them. You may have to interpret the work of your organization according to its specific functions. For example, one nonprofit agency uses volunteers to advocate in the courts on behalf of children in the foster care system. Its goal is to bring about permanent solutions to the children's situations. When this agency first secured grants from foundations and corporations, it did so for general support of its program. Finding supporters reluctant to continue providing general support once the program was launched, the staff began to write proposals for specific aspects of the agency's work, such as volunteer recruitment, volunteer training, and advocacy, thus making it easier for donors to continue to fund ongoing, core activities.

Some foundations do give general operating support. You will use the print and electronic directories, Web sites, annual reports, the foundations' own 990-PFs, and other resources described elsewhere in this book to target those that are true candidates for operating and annual support requests, if you find that your funding priorities cannot be packaged into projects. Alternatively, your general operating dollars *might* have to come from nonfoundation sources.

3. Support from individual donors and government agencies might be better sources for some of the priorities you are seeking to fund. Moreover, having a diverse base of funding support is beneficial to the financial well-being of your nonprofit agency and is important to foundation and corporate prospects. They look for the sustainability of organizations beyond receipt of their own gifts. Foundation and corporation support usually will not take the place of support from individuals in the form of personal gifts raised via face-to-face solicitation, special events, and direct mail and/or by earned income in the form of fees or dues.

You know the priorities of your organization. You have determined which ones should be developed for submission to foundations and corporations in the form of a proposal. You are now ready to move on to the proposal-writing step.

2

Developing the Master Proposal: Preparation, Tips on Writing, Overview of Components

One advantage of preparing the master proposal before you approach any funders is that all of the details will have been worked out. You will have the answers to just about any question posed to you about this project.

Another advantage is that usually you will need to customize only the cover letter, to reflect the connection between your agency and that particular funder or to take note of its specific program priorities. Few funders require a separate application form or special format.

Gathering Background Information

The first thing you will need to do in writing the master proposal is to gather the documentation for it. You will require background documentation in three areas: concept, program, and expenses.

If all of this information is not readily available to you, determine who will help you gather each type of information. If you are part of a small nonprofit with no staff, a knowledgeable board member will be the logical choice. If you are in a larger agency, there should be program and financial support staff who can help you. Once you know with whom to talk, identify the questions to ask.

This data-gathering process makes the actual writing much easier. And by involving other stakeholders in the process, it also helps key people within your agency seriously consider the project's value to the organization.

Concept

It is important that you have a good sense of how the project fits into the philosophy and mission of your agency. The need that the proposal is addressing must also be documented. These concepts must be well-articulated in the proposal. Funders want to know that a project reinforces the overall direction of an organization, and they might need to be convinced that the case for the project is compelling. You should collect background data on your organization and on the need to be addressed so that your arguments are well-documented.

Program

Here is a checklist of the program information you require:

- the nature of the project and how it will be conducted;
- the timetable for the project;
- the anticipated outcomes and how best to evaluate the results; and
- staffing and volunteer needs, including deployment of existing staff and new hires.

Expenses

You will not be able to pin down all of the expenses associated with the project until the program details and timing have been worked out. Thus, the main financial data gathering takes place after the narrative part of the master proposal has been written. However, at this stage you do need to sketch out the broad outlines of the budget to be sure that the costs are in reasonable proportion to the outcomes you anticipate. If it appears that the costs will be prohibitive, even anticipating a foundation grant, you should then scale back your plans or adjust them to remove the least cost-effective expenditures.

Deciding Who Will Write the Proposal

While gathering data, you can make the decision about who will actually write the document. You might decide to ask someone else to draft it for you. This is a tough decision. If the obvious staff member you identify to write the first draft will have to put aside some other major task, it might not be cost-effective for the agency, and you might consider whether someone else on staff is a skilled writer or a willing learner and could be freed up from routine assignments.

If you lack a staff member with the skills and time to take on the task, a volunteer or board member might be an excellent alternative. You will need to identify someone who knows the agency and writes well. You will spend substantial time with this person, helping to describe the kind of document you want. In the long run, this can be time well spent, because you now have identified a willing and skilled volunteer proposal writer.

If you have found your writer on staff or among your volunteer ranks, you are all set. The information for the proposal has been gathered, and work can commence. Should you fail to find someone this way, then an outsider will be needed. Bear in mind, before you choose this option, that the most successful proposals are often "home grown," even if they aren't perfect. A too-slick proposal obviously written by an outsider can be a real turnoff to funders.

On the other hand, while someone inside your agency will always know your organization better than a consultant, an outsider can bring objectivity to the process and may write more easily, especially with the data gathering already complete. Once the decision is made to use a consultant, you will need to make a list of prospective consultants, interview the leading candidates, check references, and make your selection.

You and the consultant will develop a contract that adequately reflects the proposed relationship. This document should include:

- details on the tasks to be performed by the consultant;
- the date when the contract becomes effective and the date of its expiration;
- a cancellation clause that can be exercised by either party within a specific number of days' notice, usually not less than 30 or more than 90 days;
- a statement that the agency owns the resulting proposal;
- information on the fee that the consultant will be paid and when it is to be paid (perhaps tying it to delivery of the product or completion of specified tasks);
- details on reimbursement of out-of-pocket expenses or on an expense advance on which the consultant may draw; and
- a provision for the contract to be signed both by the consultant and by an officer of the nonprofit.

If possible, your nonprofit organization should use legal counsel in developing the contract. At a minimum, an attorney should review the document to see that the agency's interests are protected. Seek out *pro bono* legal assistance, if need be. Do not consider oral agreements to be binding on either side. Put everything in writing.

Tips on Writing the Proposal

Regardless of who writes the proposal, grant requests are unique documents. They are unlike any other kind of writing assignment. Here are some tips for the proposal writer:

For many grantseekers, the proposal is the *only* opportunity to communicate with a foundation or corporate donor.

The written document is the one thing that remains with a funder after all the meetings and telephone calls have taken place. It must be self-explanatory. It must reflect the agency's overall image. Your proposal will educate the funder about your project and agency. It should motivate the potential funder to make a gift.

You do need to put as much care into preparing your proposal as you have put into designing the project and as you are planning to put into operating it. You have spent a fair amount of time determining priorities for raising funds and gathering the appropriate information for the proposal. The information you have collected should be thoroughly woven into an integrated whole that dramatically depicts your agency's project for the funder.

There are some basic rules that apply to all writing and a few that are unique to proposals for foundations and corporations.

Get Your Thoughts Sorted Out

A proposal must deliver critical ideas quickly and easily. Your writing must be clear if you want others to understand your project and become excited by it. It will be hard to accomplish this if you have not clarified your thoughts in advance.

This means identifying the central point of your proposal. All of your subsequent points should flow easily from it. Once you have clearly thought through the broad concepts of the proposal, you are ready to prepare an outline.

Outline What You Want to Say

You understand the need for the program. You have already gathered the facts about how it will unfold, if funded. You have identified the benchmarks of success and the financial requirements. With this information in hand, outline what should be said and in what order. If you take the time to create this outline, the process of writing will be much easier, and the resulting proposal will be stronger. Rushing to write a document without an outline only leads to frustration, confusion, and a poorly articulated proposal.

Avoid Jargon

Jargon confuses the reader and hampers his or her ability to comprehend your meaning. It impedes your style. It may be viewed as pretentious. With so much at stake in writing a proposal, it makes sense to avoid words (and acronyms) that are not generally known and to select words for their precision.

Be Compelling, but Don't Overstate Your Case

People give to people. While your proposal has to present the facts, it must let the human element shine through. Personify the issue. Tell your story with examples. Illuminate your vision so that the funder can share it with you. Don't be afraid to humanize the materials once the facts are in place. But never assume that your writing is so compelling that programmatic details are unnecessary. A number of the grantmakers interviewed for this guide indicated a preference for real-life examples to enhance the text of a proposal. Mary Gregory of the Bella Vista Foundation offers this suggestion: "Stories are critical. Tell me about the typical client and how the program will work for that person." Laura Gilbertson of the William Bingham Foundation explains: "I try to visualize the program or service. What would happen to me if I went there?"

Try to be realistic in presenting your case. Take care that in your enthusiasm you do not overstate the need, the projected outcomes, or the basic facts about your organization.

It is dangerous to promise more than you can deliver. The proposal reviewer is sure to raise questions, and the result could be damaged credibility with the funder. Worse, if the proposal is funded, and the results do not live up to the exaggerated expectations, future support is jeopardized.

Keep It Simple

In the old days, fundraisers believed that the longer the document and the more detail it had, the better it was and the more money could be requested. Today, foundation and corporate funders look for concisely presented ideas. Eliminate wordiness. Simply present the key thoughts.

Keep It Generic

As you progress through the fundraising process, you may well approach a number of different potential funders with the same or a similar proposal. Thus, it makes sense to develop a master proposal that, with certain customizing touches, can be submitted to a number of sources. Some funders today are even beginning to accept master proposals submitted online.

In some areas of the country, groups of foundations have agreed to adopt a common application form. It makes sense to inquire as to whether one exists in your geographic area and whether the funder you are applying to accepts proposals in this form. The very same careful research that goes into identifying appropriate funders pertains to contacting those that accept common application forms. Examples of common application forms can be found at the Foundation Center's World Wide Web site at http://fdncenter.org.

COMPONENTS OF A PROPOSAL

Executive Summary:	statement of your case and summary of the entire proposal	1 page
Statement of Need:	why this project is necessary	2 pages
Project Description:	nuts and bolts of how the project will be implemented and evaluated	3 pages
Budget:	financial description of the project plus explanatory notes	1 page
Organization Information:	history and governing structure of the non-profit; its primary activities, its audiences, and its services	1 page
Conclusion:	summary of the proposal's main points	2 paragraphs

Revise and Edit

Once you have completed the proposal, put it away temporarily. Then in a day or two, reread it with detachment and objectivity, if possible. Look for the logic of your arguments. Are there any holes? Move on to analyzing word choices and examining the grammar. Karen Rosa of the Altman Foundation reminds us, "Proofread the proposal package." And she notes: "Spell check has its disadvantages, since it tends to let us off the hook in terms of feeling obligated to reread every word and cannot tell us if we are using the wrong spelling entirely for the meaning of the sentence—e.g., 'it's' for 'its' or 'pier' for 'peer'." Finally, give the document to someone else to read. Select someone with well-honed communication skills, who can point out areas that remain unclear and raise unanswered questions. Ask for a critical review of the case and of the narrative flow. This last step will be most helpful in closing any gaps, in eliminating jargon, and in heightening the overall impact of the document.

A well-crafted document should result from all these hours of gathering, thinking and sifting, and writing and rewriting. Carol Robinson, former executive director of the Isaac H. Tuttle Fund, provided us with an ideal to strive for that is still very telling today: "To me a proposal is a story. You speak to the reader and tell the reader a story, something you want him/her to visualize, hear, feel. It should have dimension, shape and rhythm and, yes, it should 'sing.'" (private letter, December 30, 1985)

The following chapters include many examples to assist you in better understanding the points being made. A number of these are excerpts from actual proposals and are reprinted with permission from the issuing agency. Please note that to keep the design of the book simple, we did not reproduce these examples in their original formats.

No two proposals are precisely the same in their execution, and no single proposal is absolutely perfect. In fact, some of the examples presented here have flaws. These examples are used to underscore a specific point, but together they illustrate the more general one that flexibility on the part of the proposal writer is essential. In a winning proposal, often the nature of the issues being addressed overrides rules about format.

A full sample proposal appears in Appendix A.

3

Developing the
Master Proposal:
The Executive Summary

This first page of the proposal is the most important section of the entire document. Here you will provide the reader with a snapshot of what is to follow. Specifically, it summarizes all of the key information and is a sales document designed to convince the reader that this project should be considered for support. Be certain to include:

Problem—a brief statement of the problem or need your agency has recognized and is prepared to address (one or two paragraphs);

Solution—a short description of the project, including what will take place and how many people will benefit from the program, how and where it will operate, for how long, and who will staff it (one or two paragraphs);

Funding requirements—an explanation of the amount of grant money required for the project and what your plans are for funding it in the future (one paragraph); and

Organization and its expertise—a brief statement of the name, history, purpose, and activities of your agency and its capacity to carry out this proposal (one paragraph).

How will the executive summary be used? First, in the initial review of your request, it will enable the funder to determine that the proposal is within its guidelines. Then it is often forwarded to other staff or board members to assist in their general review of the request. If you don't provide a summary, someone at the funder's office may well do it for you and emphasize the wrong points.

Here's a tip: It is easier to write the executive summary last. You will have your arguments and key points well in mind. It should be concise. Ideally, the summary should be no longer than one page or 300 words.

Here is an example of an executive summary, taken from a proposal submitted by Good Shepherd Services to the Frances L. & Edwin L. Cummings Memorial Fund. This summary immediately identifies the financial request. It provides an excellent synopsis of the problem and the proposed solution. The use of Roman numerals is unusual.

Executive Summary

I. Good Shepherd Services is requesting a grant of $50,000 from the Frances L. & Edwin L. Cummings Memorial Fund to support South Brooklyn Community High School (SBCHS), a Good Shepherd Services/Department of Education collaboration for young people who have been excessively truant or have dropped out of school. The school was planned and implemented through funding from New Visions for Public Schools' *New Century High Schools for NYC Initiative,* which seeks to transform and improve high school education in New York City. The school builds on the successful model program that Good Shepherd operated for 22 years and includes a rigorous, standards-based, instructional program; a personalized learning environment; numerous leadership opportunities; a strong parent involvement component; and partnerships with

---

community resources to enhance the opportunities available to the students.

A grant from the Cummings Fund would support the position of an Advocate Counselor and provide educational enrichment supplies. Advocate Counselors are an integral component of our program and provide students with the support they need to achieve their educational goals, overcome personal obstacles and develop plans for long-term achievement. Educational enrichment materials offer students the resources to develop the competencies necessary for academic success.

II. SBCHS currently works with 120 students from the South Brooklyn community who have histories of extensive truancy or who have dropped out of school. SBCHS integrates two equally important components—a standards-based instructional model, and a support structure which focuses on leadership development, goal-setting and community building—into an educational community that is immersed in the best practices of youth development and focuses on students' strengths as it fosters achievement. This model helps students resolve issues that have hindered attendance and academic progress to earn their diploma and develop academic and career oriented post-graduation plans.

III. We seek to achieve the following objectives during the 2003–2004 program year:

- SBCHS will reach an enrollment of 150 students.
- The overall average attendance rate of the collective student body at SBCHS will be 75% by the end of the academic year.
- 80% of SBCHS students will participate in leadership activities.
- Of those SBCHS students targeted in the fall as eligible for graduation at the end of the academic year, 80% will graduate and receive their high school diplomas.
- 95% of SBCHS graduates will develop a plan for post-high school education, vocational training, and/or full-time employment.

IV. SBCHS directly contributes to Good Shepherd Services' overall mission through ongoing efforts to help former dropouts develop the competencies necessary for future success. SBCHS strives to help its students develop the critical skills that they will need for further education, careers, and positive family and community involvement. At the same time, the program also works to insure that students meet important developmental and personal needs. All of these efforts are deeply linked to the agency's mission of providing quality service to individuals and communities, advocating zealously for principles necessary to empower those with whom we work, and leading in the development of innovative programs that insure access to the future.

V. Our active Development Department is continuously researching private and government funding opportunities funding to sustain SBCHS activities.

Another example also comes from a proposal written for the Frances L. & Edwin L. Cummings Memorial Fund, by Teach For America • New Jersey. Note the use of italics to set off the agency's vision for the future.

PROPOSAL SUMMARY

This is a proposal to expand the presence of Teach For America in Newark and to impact the achievement levels of thousands of students in New Jersey's lowest-income communities. Teach For America is the national corps of outstanding recent college graduates of all academic majors who commit two years to teach in under-resourced urban and rural public schools. With added insight and heightened commitment, these corps members then join an active network of alumni who continue the fight to improve the educational and life prospects for all children. After nearly a decade of bringing exceptional teachers and education leaders to New Jersey's under-resourced school districts, we are launching an expansion plan to double the number of new teachers placed by 2005, significantly increasing both our short-term and long-term impact. In addition, as detailed later in this proposal, we have partnered with the Newark Public Schools on an initiative to focus our work by ensuring that all 2003 corps members will be placed in Newark (Essex County) alone.

While we have made great progress over the past nine years—placing nearly 300 corps members in New Jersey communities and building a strong program and stable organization—students in low-income areas continue to achieve significantly below their peers in high-income areas. Teach For America • New Jersey has proven, however, that with the help of dedicated corps members, students in urban public schools can achieve at high levels. As our growth requires additional funding, we are asking that the Cummings Memorial Fund commit to supporting a Teach For America growth plan that will in 2003 provide the Newark Public Schools with nearly half of its new teachers.

The plan outlined in this proposal details an expansion campaign whereby 78 corps members are teaching nearly 7,000 students in the 2002-2003 school year. The ambitious plan extends further to 2005, when 140 corps members will be teaching over 11,000 students. This will give Teach For America • New Jersey the critical mass necessary to create a significantly large force of informed, powerful leaders and advocates for change.

A grant from the Cummings Memorial Fund of $100,000, allotted over two years, will sponsor the cost of recruiting, selecting, training and providing on-going support for eight Newark corps members in each of those years, thus accounting for half of our incremental growth in each year. As we expand, we hope you will be inspired to continue supporting our efforts to realize the vision that *one day, all children in the nation will have the opportunity to attain an excellent education.*

Neither example contains every element of the ideal executive summary, but both persuasively present the case for reading further.

4

Developing the
Master Proposal:
The Statement of Need

If the funder reads beyond the executive summary, you have successfully piqued his or her interest. Your next task is to build on this
initial interest in your project by enabling the funder to understand
the problem that the project will remedy.

The statement of need will enable the reader to learn more about
the issues. It presents the facts and evidence that support the need
for the project and establishes that your nonprofit understands the
problems and therefore can reasonably address them. The information used to support the case can come from authorities in the field,
as well as from your agency's own experience.

You want the need section to be succinct, yet persuasive. Like a
good debater, you must assemble all the arguments and then present
them in a logical sequence that will readily convince the reader of

their importance. As you marshal your arguments, consider the following six points:

First, decide which facts or statistics best support the project. Be sure the data you present are accurate. There are few things more embarrassing than to have the funder tell you that your information is out of date or incorrect. Information that is too generic or broad will not help you develop a winning argument for your project. Information that does not relate to your organization or the project you are presenting will cause the funder to question the entire proposal. There should be a balance between the information presented and the scale of the program. Here is a list of possible sources to call upon when compiling facts, figures, and statistics to back up your case:

- needs assessments conducted by objective outside parties or by your own agency
- surveys—local or regional or national, conducted by your organization or by others
- focus groups with representatives of key audiences
- interviews with stakeholders
- usage statistics
- media coverage of the problem or lack of service
- reports from government agencies or other nonprofits
- demographic studies
- projections for the future, suggesting how bad things will get if this problem is not addressed, and/or how good things will be if it is.

These should all derive from authorities with impeccable credentials and be as up-to-date as possible.

An example might be helpful here. Your nonprofit organization plans to initiate a program for battered women, for which you will seek support from foundations and corporations in your community. You have impressive national statistics on hand. You can also point to an increasing number of local women and their children seeking help. However, local data is limited. Given the scope of the project and the base of potential supporters, you should probably use the more limited local information only. It is far more relevant to the interests of funders close to home. If you were to seek support from more nationally oriented funders, then the broader information would be helpful, supplemented by details based on local experience.

Second, give the reader hope. The picture you paint should not be so grim that the situation appears hopeless. The funder will wonder whether an investment in a solution will be worthwhile. Here's an example of a solid statement of need: "Breast cancer kills. But statistics prove that regular check-ups catch most breast cancer in the early stages, reducing the likelihood of death. Hence, a program to encourage preventive checkups will reduce the risk of death due to breast cancer." Avoid overstatement and overly emotional appeals.

Third, decide if you want to put your project forward as a model. This could expand the base of potential funders, but serving as a model works only for certain types of projects. Don't try to make this argument if it doesn't really fit. Funders may well expect your agency to follow through with a replication plan if you present your project as a model.

If the decision about a model is affirmative, you should document how the problem you are addressing occurs in other communities. Be sure to explain how your solution could be a solution for others as well.

Fourth, determine whether it is reasonable to portray the need as acute. You are asking the funder to pay attention to your proposal because either the problem you address is worse than others or the solution you propose makes more sense than others. Here is an example of a balanced but weighty statement: "Drug abuse is a national problem. Each day, children all over the country die from drug overdose. In the South Bronx the problem is worse. More children die here than any place else. It is an epidemic. Hence, our drug prevention program is needed more in the South Bronx than in any other part of the city."

Fifth, decide whether you can demonstrate that your program addresses the need differently or better than other projects that preceded it. It is often difficult to describe the need for your project without being critical of the competition. But you must be careful not to do so. Being critical of other nonprofits will not be well received by the funder. It may cause the funder to look more carefully at your own project to see why you felt you had to build your case by demeaning others. The funder may have invested in these other projects or may begin to consider them, now that you have brought them to its attention.

If possible, you should make it clear that you are cognizant of, and on good terms with, others doing work in your field. Keep in mind that today's funders are very interested in collaboration. They may even ask why you are not collaborating with those you view as key competitors. So at the least you need to describe how your work complements, but does not duplicate, the work of others.

Sixth, avoid circular reasoning. In circular reasoning, you present the absence of your solution as the actual problem. Then your solution is offered as the way to solve the problem. For example, the circular reasoning for building a community swimming pool might go like this: "The problem is that we have no pool in our community. Building a pool will solve the problem." A more persuasive case would cite what a pool has meant to a neighboring community, permitting it to offer recreation, exercise, and physical therapy programs. The statement might refer to a survey that underscores the target audience's planned usage of the facility and conclude with the connection between the proposed usage and potential benefits to enhance life in the community.

To make your need statement compelling, you'll want to put a human face on the problem. There are a number of ways you might do this:

- use anecdotes, succinctly related
- provide real-life examples (with fictitious names if need be) to make those you serve come alive
- supply actual quotes from those who have benefited or will benefit from your services
- emphasize the needs of those you serve, not your own
- always make the funder feel that there is hope that the problem will be solved.

The statement of need does not have to be long and involved. Short, concise information captures the reader's attention. This is the case in the following example from a proposal for the National Hemophilia Foundation.

STATEMENT OF NEED

As many as 3 million people in the United States are living with bleeding disorders. Despite advances in technology and treatment and all of the medical milestones scientists have achieved, people with bleeding disorders continue to live with the threat of a spontaneous, potentially fatal hemorrhage due to the inability of the blood to clot. On top of the difficulty of managing a chronic disease on a daily basis, many individuals also suffer from complications of bleeding disorders. In the late 70s and early 80s, about half of the people living with hemophilia in the United States contracted HIV through contaminated blood products; many have since died. According to data from the Centers for Disease Control and Prevention, an estimated 44% of people with hemophilia have contracted the hepatitis C virus. Another frequent complication of hemophilia is joint damage, which is the result of bleeding into the joints.

The very best medical treatment available today still means painful infusions once or twice a week for the entire span of an individual's life and can cost an average of $150,000 per year for an individual with severe hemophilia (60% of all cases are severe hemophilia). The collective cost of that treatment to the population of people with bleeding disorders is extraordinarily high—more than $1.7 billion per year. The cost of medication can threaten and even overtake lifetime health insurance limits, leaving families burdened with exorbitant out-of-pocket medical expenses and insufficient healthcare coverage. Furthermore, current treatments are not a cure, and many people with bleeding disorders still suffer from painful, debilitating joint bleeds and a variety of other complications that severely impede their quality of life.

In addition to the difficulties of living with a bleeding disorder, on an individual level, families and other caregivers are also deeply affected by the demands of the disease and have unique needs, such as: ensuring adequate health insurance coverage; making decisions about the most appropriate treatment; addressing the individual's emotional response to living with a chronic health problem, as well as the emotional responses of other family members; and learning to support the individual living with the disease in achieving a balance between leading an active life and protecting his or her well-being.

The next example comes from a proposal to the New York Foundation submitted by the Center for Family Representation (CFR). Since this is a request from a local agency to a grantmaker based in the same geographic area, the need section relies appropriately on local data and information.

CFR was founded in May of 2002 in response to the crisis in legal representation available for parents in New York City's Family Courts. This crisis is the result of a severe shortage in the attorneys available to represent parents as well as the absence of an institutional provider to deliver sustained interdisciplinary advocacy necessary to quickly and safely reunify parents with their children. The lack of a multi-service provider has left parents without a consistent voice in the many venues in which child welfare reform is developed. Importantly, there is no organization consistently available to parents *prior to* their family court involvement that can assist them in avoiding the disruption of their families in the first instance, or who can continue to represent them in court with the full panoply of resources necessary to effectively and expeditiously resolve their cases.

Despite many calls for reform, the primary source of parents' attorneys remains disperse solo practitioners who are members of the assigned counsel panel. Most commentators on the crisis conclude that assigned counsel need enhancements such as access to social workers, paralegals and investigators, and more opportunities for training and "back up" legal and appellate support. Interdisciplinary representation is widely regarded as critical to effective work with families who come into contact with the child welfare system and the Family Court, as is the need for parents to have assistance in between court appearances, or following the disposition on a case. However, panel attorneys are only assigned for one proceeding at a time; the attorney's connection to the parent ceases when the case ends, even though a parent's children remain in foster care for what is typically twelve more months until another proceeding begins.

The lack of meaningful assistance between court appearances and following disposition has grave consequences for families, because recent changes in the law mean that many agencies move to terminate a parent's rights more quickly. Despite the urgency created by this change, parents lack advocates to attend important agency meetings, to assist them in securing treatment, or to monitor interim or final orders made by the court which typically govern an agency's obligations regarding such critical issues as visiting and services, but which are often not followed. Even if a parent is aware that an agency is not fulfilling its obligations, lack of access to an attorney means that motions are not made in court to cure the problems. This situation is particularly acute for parents who have been incarcerated. Where adjournments of several months are common, a family's ability to safely reunify is tragically compromised by the lack of seamless advocacy.

The families who come to the attention of ACS and the Family Court are overwhelmingly people of color living in poverty. 70% of the children in foster care come from the poorest 17 community districts in the city. In January 2001, ACS reported that less than 5% of the children in foster care were white. As of January 2000, 93% of Family Court users were reported as "nonwhite." Many have had more than one contact with child welfare and/or the family court. In addition to whatever issues have brought a family to the attention of the Family Court, the challenges inherent in living in poverty make it likely that many of these families will have problems requiring collateral legal assistance and social work expertise.

A final example comes from a proposal submitted by the Appalachian Citizens Law Center to the Public Welfare Foundation. It paints a dramatic picture of the situation that needs addressing and its impact on local communities.

As coal mining has changed from underground mines in the 1950s to the huge surface strip mines and mountaintop removal operations of today, the amount of environmental destruction and harm to local communities has increased. Often these mines encompass several hundred acres along the ridges above communities located along the creeks in the hollows between the mountains. Furthermore in the 1990s, eastern Kentucky alone lost 10,000 mining jobs because of mechanization. While employment levels have decreased, coal production has increased due to more blasting and demolition equipment.

The burden of coal mining to Appalachian communities is more than economic. Drainage seeps into the aquifers, making well water toxic. This can destroy the only water supply for entire communities. The vibrations from blasting rumble along like earthquakes, causing house foundations to crack and shift. Dust from coal haul roads covers the nearby communities, creating problems for anyone unlucky enough to have a breathing problem, particularly for children with asthma, the elderly, and miners with black lung disease. Overloaded coal trucks are too heavy for roads and cause cracks and potholes, making roads unsafe for residents.

As you can see from all three examples, the need statement begins the process whereby the organization builds its case and tells its story. This process continues in the next section of the proposal, which describes how the project will address the need.

5

Developing the
Master Proposal:
The Project Description

In this section, describe the nuts and bolts of the project in a way that gets the reader excited about it, while making a compelling case for the approach you have adopted. It is worth stating right up front that your plan is not written in stone. It might change based on feedback on your proposal and the experience you gain through implementation. It is not worth putting your organization in a defensive position in negotiating with grantmakers, and you certainly don't want to surprise a funder if in the project's final report you state that you changed your approach.

This section of your proposal should have five subsections: objectives, methods, staffing/administration, evaluation, and sustainability. Together, objectives and methods dictate staffing and administrative requirements. They then become the focus of the evaluation to assess the results of the project. The project's sustainability flows directly from its success, hence its ability to attract other support. The five subsections present an interlocking picture of the total project.

Objectives

Objectives are the measurable outcomes of the program. They help delineate your methods. Your objectives must be tangible, specific, concrete, measurable, and achievable in a specified time period. Grantseekers often confuse objectives with goals, which are conceptual and more abstract. For the purpose of illustration, here is the goal of a project with a subsidiary objective:

Goal: Our afterschool program will help children read better.

Objective: Our afterschool remedial education program will assist 50 children in improving their reading scores by one grade level as demonstrated on standardized reading tests administered after participating in the program for six months.

The goal in this case is abstract: improving reading, while the objective is much more specific. It is achievable in the short term (six months) and measurable (improving 50 children's reading scores by one grade level).

With competition for dollars so great, well-articulated objectives are increasingly critical to a proposal's success.

Calling upon a different example, there are at least four types of objectives:

1. Behavioral—A human action is anticipated.
   Example: Fifty of the 70 children participating will learn to swim.

2. Performance—A specific time frame within which a behavior will occur, at an expected proficiency level, is anticipated.
   Example: Fifty of the 70 children will learn to swim within six months and will pass a basic swimming

proficiency test administered by a Red Cross–certified lifeguard.

3. Process—The manner in which something occurs is an end in itself.
   Example: We will document the teaching methods utilized, identifying those with the greatest success.

4. Product—A tangible item will result.
   Example: A manual will be created to be used in teaching swimming to this age and proficiency group in the future.

In any given proposal, you will find yourself setting forth one or more of these types of objectives, depending on the nature of your project. Be certain to present the objectives very clearly. Make sure that they do not become lost in verbiage and that they stand out on the page. You might, for example, use numbers, bullets, or indentations to denote the objectives in the text. Above all, be realistic in setting objectives. Don't promise what you can't deliver. Remember, the funder will want to be told in the final report that the project actually accomplished these objectives.

The example that follows is from a proposal to the Hyams Foundation, Inc., from Women Express/*Teen Voices*. It is a very brief statement of the proposed project's objectives, presented in bulleted format.

Outcomes

- 3 cycles of 8 trainings to provide mentors with specific skills including journalism, publishing, media impact and clinical training covering teen issues.
- 25 trained mentors working with Teen Editors during the three mentoring sessions (summer, fall, spring)
- 3 mentors will work for the full year
- 15–20% of mentors are women of color

Another example is from the Hathaway Brown School's proposal to the Cleveland Foundation. It delivers a clear statement of objectives for a project and makes ample use of bolding.

Objectives of The ASPIRE Program

To create a **community of students and teachers** that values the excitement of the learning process, the importance of risk-taking, and the necessity for responsible leadership

- To prepare an intelligent, self-motivated, and creative group of **middle school girls** who may be limited in opportunity to become **leaders in a multicultural world**
  - ⇒ By developing a **partnership with under-resourced Cleveland-area public schools**
  - ⇒ By creating a **tuition-free summer enrichment program** for a group of racially and ethnically diverse low-income middle school girls
  - ⇒ By offering opportunities for **personal exploration and experiential learning**

- To **foster a love for teaching** in a diverse group of college and high school students
  - ⇒ By **building a network** with leading colleges and universities
  - ⇒ By designing an **effective and highly personalized teacher-training route** that inspires talented individuals to pursue the teaching profession
  - ⇒ By **providing prospective teachers with support** as they invent, explore, and experiment in the classroom

Methods

By means of the objectives, you have explained to the funder what will be achieved by the project. The methods section describes the specific activities that will take place to achieve the objectives. It might be helpful to divide our discussion of methods into the following: how, when, and why.

How: This is the detailed description of what will occur from the time the project begins until it is completed. Your methods should match the previously stated objectives. In our example about teaching 50 children to swim, appropriate methods would describe: 1) how the youngsters will be recruited, 2) how they will be taught to enhance their skills, and 3) how their swimming skills will be measured. There would be no reason to describe an extraneous activity like helping the parents learn to enjoy swimming with their children, because using swimming to bring the family together in wholesome exercise is not a stated objective of the project.

In the next example from Habitat for Humanity's proposal to the Meadows Foundation, we learn how the agency will implement its project.

Description of the Proposed Program

Due to the tremendous need for affordable housing in San Antonio, Habitat for Humanity will be constructing an 88-unit single-family development in City Council District 6 on San Antonio's west side. This development will affordably house more than 340 people who are in need of decent and affordable housing. Approximately 18 acres of land is currently vacant and undeveloped; therefore, no people will be displaced as a result of the development. Units in this development will be built on approximately 5,000 square-foot lots. Habitat for Humanity of San Antonio (HFHSA) proposes to begin infrastructure development in mid-2003 and begin construction of homes in the first quarter of 2004, with all units completed by the end of 2005.

The 18-acre tract is located on the west side of San Antonio. It is in close proximity to other areas in which we have built Habitat for Humanity homes. The planned development is located next to a well-kept municipal park complete with softball fields. It provides our future homeowners with a great place for their children to play and space to congregate and meet new neighbors. A community of single-family houses is nearby.

With a capacity of 30+ houses completed annually (we are scheduled to build 51 houses this year), HFHSA has the capacity to build out all 88 units in this development as accomplished in our previous two large-scale subdivisions.

The Center for Family Representation's proposal explains its plans for the Community Advocacy Team (CAT). Note highly specific listing of anticipated outcomes.

Strategies Which Will Be Used to Implement the CAT and Benefits of the CAT:

- Parents served by CWOP and WPA will self-identify their need for assistance from the CAT when ACS involvement begins or when they identify any need for advocacy or information regarding a foster care agency or an anticipated or actual family court case;
- Through ongoing training provided by the CAT, including the parent advocates, CAT members will work with parents and staff at WPA and CWOP to further assess client needs and provide regular information on how best to engage the child welfare and family court systems;
- When referred prior to family court involvement, parents would receive necessary information on available services, as well as on their legal rights, without the fear that disclosure would result in the removal of their children prematurely;
- At critical points in the child protective process which usually precedes family court involvement, CAT social workers, paralegals and parent advocates will provide referrals and act as an advocate for the parent at ACS meetings and conferences regarding the family;
- Administrative remedies, such as those that are available to a parent who is improperly denied services, will be pursued by CAT attorneys;
- If a petition is filed, the parent would come to court with an interdisciplinary CAT that is familiar with both her family and the resources available to her in the community and could immediately begin to work effectively both within and outside the court process;
- For parents who lack counsel because one stage of their case has ended, but another has yet to begin, CAT could quickly intervene with the agency, pursue

interim appeals or other trial remedies, and be
available to prevent further dilution of the parent's
relationship with her children; in the case of an
incarcerated parent, such resources would be
particularly critical;

- CAT members would be available for ongoing ad hoc
legal and social work assistance by telephone, email or
conferences, to members of CWOP and clients of WPA.

The following outcomes will be achieved: parents will work
more effectively with ACS and will more easily access the services necessary to avoid removal of their children; more families
will be diverted from court altogether, but where a proceeding is
begun, the CAT's prior and ongoing relationship with parents
will result in fewer removals or shorter foster care stays for the
children; in these instances and in those in which the CAT
receives the client after a proceeding is in progress, CAT intervention will result in cases being resolved more expeditiously
and more often in ways that promote reunification, such as
strengthened visiting arrangements; parent advocate positions
will provide parents with significant employment and leadership roles in reforming legal representations and child welfare.

Think about how you can most readily construct a logical
sequence from each objective to its relevant method. This can be
accomplished in a number of ways, some relating simply to visual
placement on the page.

One means of organizing this section is to write out each objective
and to list beneath it the method(s) that will make the objective possible. For example, it might look like this:

Objective: to recruit 70 children

Methods:

- Put up signs in the Y.
- Go to each school and address classes on the fun of
swimming.
- Put ads in the local paper.
- Enclose a flyer about the program with the next mailer
sent out to each family in the community.

The methods should match the magnitude of the objectives. Once you are sure that each objective has related methods that describe how the objective will be achieved, you should check that the emphasis given each method matches the importance of the related objective. In our swimming example, recruitment of 70 children is probably the least important objective; demonstrating that 50 of them can pass the Red Cross test is more critical. To match the magnitude of the objectives with appropriate detail about the project, more emphasis should be placed on the testing than on recruiting. (This refining and highlighting of information will enable the reader to understand the project and to have confidence in your agency.)

The methods should appear doable; otherwise, you lose credibility. For example, if the swimming course is to be taught by an Olympic swimmer who remains anonymous, the reader might question whether the organization can deliver what it has promised. However, if the Olympic star is identified by name and has already agreed to run the program, the reader will likely be convinced.

When: The methods section should present the order and timing for the various tasks. It might make sense to provide a timetable so that the reader does not have to map out the sequencing on his or her own. The timetable could look like this one, excerpted from the Hathaway Brown School proposal.

Project Timeline

Phase 1: Summer–Fall 2000

- Created a vision for ASPIRE by seeking connections with the Cleveland community and others involved in similar work

Phase 2: Spring 2001

- Wrote grants for start-up costs

Phase 3: Summer 2001–Spring 2002

- Began to build network with partner schools and other similar programs, developed program structure, continued fundraising, and launched initial summer program

---

Phase 4: Summer 2002

- Pilot Summer Program began with 36 rising sixth grade girls and 16 faculty/staff

Phase 5: Fall 2002–Spring 2003

- Evaluated and refined program
- Launched year-round component
- Expanded and refined partner network of schools
- Developed video and Web site
- Continued fundraising for second and third year costs and endowment

Phase 6: Summer 2003

- Second phase of the Summer Program begins with 70 students (rising sixth and seventh students) and 24 faculty/staff

Phase 7: Fall 2003–Spring 2004

- Strengthen and refine partner network of schools (elementary and middle schools)
- Continue year round program development (possibly pilot partnership program with local organization)
- Create an advisory committee to facilitate long-term fundraising plan
- Design meaningful year 3 program for rising eighth graders
- Develop effective evaluation methods
- Refine transportation structure
- Establish stronger programs for ASPIRE parents
- Develop ASPIRE alumni program structure

Phase 8: Summer 2004

- Summer program begins with full capacity—100–105 students (rising sixth, seventh and eighth graders) and 32 faculty/staff

Another presentation of a solid work plan comes from a proposal submitted to the Flinn Foundation by the Hualapai Tribal Health Department. The time line depicts a one-year project.

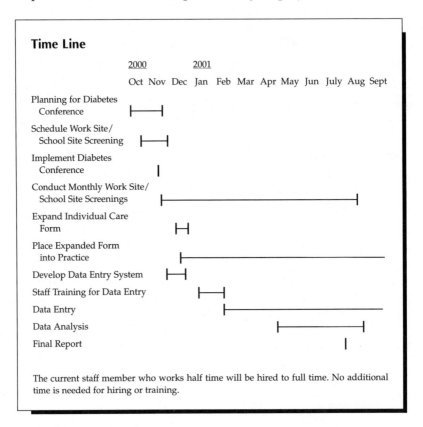

Time Line

	2000			2001								
	Oct	Nov	Dec	Jan	Feb	Mar	Apr	May	Jun	July	Aug	Sept

Planning for Diabetes Conference

Schedule Work Site/ School Site Screening

Implement Diabetes Conference

Conduct Monthly Work Site/ School Site Screenings

Expand Individual Care Form

Place Expanded Form into Practice

Develop Data Entry System

Staff Training for Data Entry

Data Entry

Data Analysis

Final Report

The current staff member who works half time will be hired to full time. No additional time is needed for hiring or training.

The timetable tells the reader "when" and provides another summary of the project that supports the rest of the methods section.

Why: You need to defend your chosen methods, especially if they are new or unorthodox. Why will the planned work lead to the outcomes you anticipate? You can answer this question in a number of ways, including using examples of other projects that work and expert testimony.

The methods section enables the reader to visualize the implementation of the project. It should convince the reader that your agency knows what it is doing, thereby establishing credibility.

Staffing/Administration

In describing the methods, you will have mentioned staffing for the project. You now need to devote a few sentences to discussing the number of staff, their qualifications, and specific assignments. Details about individual staff members involved in the project can be included either as part of this section or in the appendix, depending on the length and importance of this information.

"Staffing" can refer to volunteers or to consultants, as well as to paid staff. Most proposal writers do not develop staffing sections for projects that are primarily volunteer-run. Describing tasks that volunteers will undertake, however, can be most helpful to the proposal reader. Such information underscores the value added by the volunteers and the cost-effectiveness of the project.

For a project with paid staff, be certain to describe which staff will work full time and which will work part time on the project. Identify staff already employed by your nonprofit and those to be recruited specifically for the project. How will you free up the time of an already fully deployed individual?

Salary and project costs are affected by the qualifications of the staff. Delineate the practical experience you require for key staff, as well as level of expertise and educational background. If an individual has already been selected to direct the program, summarize his or her credentials and include a brief biographical sketch in the appendix. A strong project director can help influence a grant decision.

Explain anything unusual about the proposed staffing for the project. It is better to include such information in the proposal narrative than to have the funder raise questions once the proposal review begins.

Three samples of staffing sections follow. The first is part of a proposal from Groundwork.

STAFF

Groundwork is led by a management team with expertise in nonprofit and commercial enterprise development. **Richard Buery,** Groundwork's co-founder and Executive Director, most recently co-founded and directed iMentor, a technology education and mentoring program, and has previous experience practicing civil rights law, teaching, and managing community-based youth development programs. A native of East New York and the son of a long time teacher at East New York High School, Richard has a deep commitment to community and first hand experience with the challenges faced by the young people Groundwork serves. **Andrea Schorr,** also a Groundwork co-founder, is the organization's Associate Executive Director for Programs and Evaluation. She previously founded the L. E. A. P. Computer Learning Center, one of the nation's first community technology centers for children, and was an associate at the Morino Institute, a foundation that manages Venture Philanthropy Partners, a Washington, D.C. region venture philanthropy fund. **Richard Souto,** Associate Executive Director for Finance and Operations, has a background in corporate development and private investment with several early stage health care and telecommunications companies, and has extensive volunteer experience with youth serving nonprofits including Youth Tech Entrepreneurs and the National Foundation for Teaching Entreneurship. **Erica Ahdoot,** Director of Support Services, has extensive experience with youth and family mental health services in youth development settings. Erica was recently employed at the Vera Institute for Justice, where she provided individual and family based substance abuse treatment for youth in the New York State juvenile justice system. **Darren Isom,** Program Director for Groundwork for Youth, brings for-profit and non-profit experiences to Groundwork. Most recently, he was Director of Global Logistics for CSI Complex Systems, Inc., an international trade finance group, and previously he was a teacher and administrator for Summerbridge, an academic enrichment program for urban youth.

Groundwork also benefits from an engaged Board of Directors including individuals from the corporate and foundation world.

A request to the Altman Foundation submitted by East Side House has a simple, straightforward staffing section.

Project READY Staff

East Side House's Youth Leadership Program Director, Melissa Chiodi, will oversee the entire Project READY program and other youth leadership activities at MHV Prep. Ms. Chiodi will be further supported by an East Side House staff team consisting of: 1) a full-time Social Worker; 2) Two Education Counselors—1 full-time and 1 part-time; and 3) two part-time Tutors. The Project Ready staffing plan further supports the two-tiered structure and will act as a bridge between the school day activities (for the ninth grade students) and the after school activities. By interfacing with the school day staff about college issues, the Project READY staff team ensures that students receive a comprehensive, "wrap-around" of services.

And finally, here is the staffing section from the Arts in Progress proposal to the Hyams Foundation, Inc.

Staff

Consistent with Arts In Progress' goals of shaping young lives with the power of positive relationships, its programs are staffed by professional artist/teachers who are both dynamic educators and compelling role models. These staff include:

- Nicole Smith—As Director of Theater Education at AIP, Nicole brings a unique combination of education and curriculum design experience, professional development, and direct service with urban children and youth both within and outside of school to the Teen Arts Center and the agency's school-based programs.
- Ben Sloat—As Director of AIP's Digital Photography program, Mr. Sloat brings an MFA, from the Museum School, a youthful enthusiasm, and fresh experience over the past several years as a photographer and teacher to the Teen Arts Center.

- Dirk Adams—An accomplished media artist, Mr. Adams brings an MFA in the Visual and Performing Arts and a wealth of artistic and teaching experiences over the past four years to the TAC.

In addition to being accomplished artists, AIP artist/teachers have a passion and commitment to working with urban children and youth, developing the powerful relationships that can help to shape lives, influence choices, and illuminate a positive path to the future.

Describe for the reader your plans for administering the project. This is especially important in a large operation, if more than one agency is collaborating on the project, or if you are using a fiscal agent. It needs to be crystal clear who is responsible for financial management, project outcomes, and reporting.

Evaluation

Keep in mind that most grantmakers today do require an evaluation component as part of your proposal. This is so important that many specifically indicate what their expectations regarding evaluation are in advance of your making an application. This information often will be found in their guidelines and/or on their Web sites. If it is not clear what kind of evaluation plan you need to construct, be sure to ask the prospective funder before you proceed with your proposal. An evaluation plan should not be considered only after the project is over; it should be built into the project. At this stage foundation and corporate prospects hope to find clear-cut, measurable and realistic plans to determine whether or not your project succeeds. They need enough details to determine specific performance objectives and how they will be met. Including an evaluation plan in your proposal indicates that you take your objectives seriously and want to know how well you have achieved them. Evaluation is also a sound management tool. Like strategic planning, it helps a nonprofit refine and improve its program. To quote Marci Lu of the Cleveland Foundation, "We ask for an evaluation plan so that a mind shift can occur among nonprofit organizations. Our grantees need to develop the habit of collecting and analyzing data to continually improve and modify their programs. The evaluation is really for the nonprofit, not for the foundation." An evaluation can often be the best means for others to learn from your experience in conducting the project.

Match the evaluation to the project. If you are asking for funds to buy an additional personal computer, it is not necessary to develop an elaborate plan to assess its impact on your operation. But if you have requested $100,000 to encourage people to have blood tests for Lyme disease, you should have a mechanism to determine whether the project's activities achieved your goals and objectives.

Many projects will have rather obvious evaluation procedures built into them. An art institution working on audience development, a settlement house providing an after-school program to disadvantaged children, or a health clinic offering preventive immunization will not spend a great deal of money and time evaluating their respective projects. The number of people served will be the major indicator of the success of these projects.

Not all funders require a formal evaluation; some want monitoring reports only. In this case, it is up to you to decide whether a formal evaluation is an essential component of the project. Many of the funders interviewed for this book, however, told us that a sound evaluation plan, based on measurable outcomes, is the hallmark of a successful proposal. And, you will want to remain flexible about precisely how you will evaluate your project because once the grant is awarded, funding representatives may want to further shape the evaluation.

By way of an evaluation component, a proposal from the Canal Community Alliance to the Bothin Foundation indicates the relationship between outcomes and evaluation in a chart-like format.

Purpose, Goals, Activities, Outcomes and Evaluation

The purpose of Radio Canal is twofold: 1) it is an innovative job training and leadership development program for at-risk, low income youth; and, 2) it is a vital community resource for disseminating information about local news, cultural and community events, jobs and health information, and other important consumer information to non-English and limited-English speaking residents of Marin county. We have three simple goals: 1) Conduct regular Latino radio programs for our community; 2) Provide job skills training and leadership development to local, at-risk, low-income youth, and 3) Increase community involvement and listener satisfaction.

Goals	Activities	Outcomes	Evaluation
Goal 1—Conduct regular Latino radio programs for our community	1. Develop programs 2. Test program's effectiveness 3. Air programs	1. 1,200 listeners 2. At least 10 hours of airtime per week	1. On the air surveys asking listeners to call in responding to programming as well as overall satisfaction with radio programming. The standard measurement for listeners set by national public radio is 1 call-in = 100 listeners 2. Call-in log reviews 3. Participant accomplishment assessment 4. Mentor observation and feedback 5. Program director's observation and feedback 6. Participant storytelling
Goal 2—Provide job skills training and leadership development to local, at-risk, low income youth	1. Recruit mentors and interns 2. Set individual training goals with each participant 3. Train and support mentors 4. Provide mentors, who encourage and support interns, to use newly acquired skills	1. 85% of all participants will accomplish 100% of what they set out to do 2. 20 trained youth	
Goal 3—Increase community involvement and listeners satisfaction	1. Air programs by, for and about the people in the broadcast area 2. Outreach to and involve community in programming 3. Create connections with community grassroots groups	1. Increase number of community members involved 2. 80% of those surveyed will be satisfied with radio show	

Canal Community Alliance Proposal 2003

Here is the evaluation section of a proposal submitted by Family Focus to the William Randolph Hearst Foundation.

Outcomes and Evaluations

Family Focus, Inc. has developed ten desired outcomes for its family support programs:

- reduction in rates of subsequent pregnancies
- healthy growth and development of program participants and their children
- enhanced self-sufficiency in academic career
- healthy parent-child relationships
- improved health and emotional development of parents
- increased parents' competence to maintain children's health
- enhanced self-sufficiency in family life
- enhanced ability of parents to support children's education and school readiness
- delay of first pregnancy
- increased school success for 80 percent of participants

Each center and program works to achieve outcomes appropriate for its target population (i.e., infants, school-age children, pregnant and parenting teens, adult parents, etc.) through information and support groups, home visiting, parent-child activities, after-school programs, case management, literacy courses, mentoring, and community outreach. In addition to the individual center evaluation tools and procedures, Family Focus uses an outcome-based program evaluation that helps assess program effectiveness. From the ten desired outcomes, staff members identify those for which their programs are responsible. Staff members ensure that the programs are providing the appropriate content, experiences, and services to reach the intended outcomes. Family Focus uses established evaluation tools to determine the effectiveness of its programming. The Adult/Adolescent Parent Inventory (AAPI) and the 40 Developmental Assessments (DA) are two examples of the measurement tools being used for parents and non-parenting youth, respectively.

Pre-participation tests are used to determine risks to children and unhealthy behaviors by measuring a variety of factors including inappropriate expectations of children, belief in corporal punishment as a means of discipline, constructive use of time, and other high-risk behavior patterns. Post-participant tests are used to determine the effects of program involvement on these behaviors and attitudes. Results help staff members determine if and what program changes need to be made to accomplish the necessary outcomes.

The next excerpt is the project evaluation from the Good Shepherd Services proposal.

Project Evaluation

We view assessment as an ongoing improvement process for all members of our learning community. As such, the youth members of our school community participate in assessing the school through satisfaction surveys, process oriented feedback in small groups and community meetings, and participation in school wide committees and leadership structures. All of this data is then incorporated into our school planning and continuous improvement efforts. In addition, over the past several years, in collaboration with our IT and Quality Improvement Departments, we have continued to evaluate and implement our strategic systems that monitor students' progress in meeting desired outcomes in attendance, academic achievement, and the preparation of post-graduate plans. We now utilize several new recording forms and a computer database to track results and generate aggregate outcome reports after each three-month cycle.

There are two types of formal evaluation. One measures the product; the other analyzes the process. Either or both might be appropriate to your project. The approach you choose will depend on the nature of the project and its objectives. For either type, you will need to describe the manner in which evaluative information will be collected and how the data will be analyzed. You should present your plan for how the evaluation and its results will be reported and the audiences to which it will be directed. For example, it might be used internally or be shared with the funder, or it might deserve a wider audience. A funder might have an opinion about the scope of this dissemination.

Should in-house staff or outside consultants conduct a formal evaluation? Staff may not have sufficient distance from the project to be objective. An outside person can bring objectivity to the project, but consultants may be costly and require time to learn about your agency and the project. Again, the nature of the project and of the evaluation may well determine the answer to this question. In any case, the evaluation section needs to strike a balance between familiarity with the project and objectivity about the product or process.

Sustainability

A clear message from grantmakers today is that grantseekers will be expected to demonstrate in very concrete ways the long-term financial viability of the project to be funded and of the nonprofit organization itself. Most of the grantmakers we interviewed indicated that they look for lists of current and prospective donors among the attachments to a proposal. This is high on the list of items they expect grantseekers to provide. Peter Bird of the Frist Foundation has this to say: "Sustainability is the Achilles' heel in many proposals. The organization paints itself into a corner and then goes to the grantmaker for help."

It stands to reason that most grantmakers will not want to take on a permanent funding commitment to a particular agency. Rather, funders will want you to prove either that your project is finite (with start-up and ending dates); or that it is capacity-building (that it will contribute to the future self-sufficiency of your agency and/or enable it to expand services that might be revenue generating); or that it will make your organization attractive to other funders in the future. With the new trend toward adopting some of the investment principles of venture capital groups to the practice of philanthropy, evidence of fiscal sustainability becomes a highly sought-after characteristic of the successful grant proposal.

It behooves you to be very specific about current and projected funding streams, both earned income and fundraised, and about the base of financial support for your nonprofit. Here is an area where it is important to have backup figures and prognostications at the ready, in case a prospective funder asks for these. Some grantmakers, of course, will want to know who else will be receiving a copy of this same proposal. You should not be shy about sharing this information with the funder.

What follows is a brief statement regarding projected sustainability from the East Side House proposal to the Altman Foundation.

SUSTAINABILITY

Project READY is supported by East Side House's aggressive fundraising plan that includes the following components:

- **Foundation and Corporate Grant Seeking** which includes aggressive outreach to appropriate foundation and corporate prospects to help underwrite special needs and projects;

- **Major Donor Cultivation** to develop and secure an individual donor base with the capacity to have significant impact on East Side House's activities;

- **Annual Benefit Events** such as the winter Antique Show and the Spring Auto Show, both of which net income to help underwrite operating costs;

- **Direct Mail** to capture others in the greater New York community to help underwrite operating costs; and

- **Government Grant Seeking** which includes applying to appropriate government requests for proposals.

And here is a sustainability plan from Arts in Progress' proposal to the Hyams Foundation, Inc.

> The programs of Arts In Progress have enjoyed a diverse funding base over the years, with public funds for the arts combining with public education funds and the resources of individuals, foundations, and corporations to support the wide array of agency program efforts. In 2003, the agency is completing its multi-phase build-out of the Teen Arts Center and its adjacent office space, combining over $500,000 in public and private investment to fully equip 10,000 square feet of office and program space. The agency's commitment to continuing to support its programming with a mix of revenue sources is unwavering, yet traditional sources of support for school programs, like Chapter 636 funds have been lost in recent years. Advocacy and continuous fund development from a variety of sources will help to fill this gap. Strategic funding goals include tapping public education funds for basic skills to support the agency's renewed efforts of creatively using the arts to build literacy and writing skills, while youth development goals can be addressed through public funding streams like public health, as new after-school revenue streams are also explored. Finally, despite the reality of providing services in the heart of Boston's poorest neighborhoods, AIP is implementing a fee scale for programs this year asking families to partially offset the burdens sustained by recent cuts in funding for the arts and education.

6

Developing the Master Proposal: The Budget

The project description provides the picture of your proposal in words. The budget further refines that picture with numbers. A well-crafted budget adds greatly to the proposal reviewer's understanding of your project.

The budget for your proposal may be as simple as a one-page statement of projected expenses. Or your proposal may require a more complex presentation, perhaps a spreadsheet including projected support and revenue and notes explaining various items of expense or revenue.

Expense Budget

As you prepare to assemble the budget, go back through the proposal narrative and make a list of all personnel and nonpersonnel items related to the operation of the project. Be sure that you list not only new costs that will be incurred if the project is funded but also any ongoing expenses for items that will be allocated to the project. Then get the relevant numbers from the person in your agency who is responsible for keeping the books. You may need to estimate the proportions of your agency's ongoing expenses that should be charged to the project and any new costs, such as salaries for project personnel not yet hired. Put the costs you have identified next to each item on your list.

It is accepted practice to include as line items in your project budget any operating costs of the agency that will be specifically devoted to running the project. Most commonly, these are the costs of supervision and of occupancy. If the project is large relative to the organization as a whole, these line items might also include telephone, utilities, office supplies, and computer-related expenses. For instance, if one of three office phone lines will be devoted to the project, one-third of the monthly cost of maintaining phone service could legitimately be listed as a project cost.

In addition, most expense budgets include a line called "overhead," which allows the project to bear a portion of the administrative costs, often called supporting services, of your operation. Such items as the bookkeeper's salary, board meeting expenses, the annual audit, and the cost of operating your personnel department might be included in the overhead figure. These costs are not directly attributable to the project but can be allocated to it based on the notion that the project should bear some of the costs of the host organization.

Most groups use a formula for allocating overhead costs to projects, usually based on the percentage of the total project budget to the total organizational budget or to its total salary line. For example, if the project budget is one-tenth the size of the total budget, it could be expected to bear one-tenth of the administrative overhead costs. Funders may have policies regarding the percentage of overhead that they will allow in a project budget. Some do not allow any overhead at all to be included. If possible, you should find out about the overhead policy before submitting your proposal to a particular foundation, because you may need to explain to that funder how you will cover overhead costs from other sources.

Your list of budget items and the calculations you have done to arrive at a dollar figure for each item should be summarized on worksheets. You should keep these to remind yourself how the numbers were developed. These worksheets can be useful as you continue to develop the proposal and discuss it with funders; they are also a valuable tool for monitoring the project once it is under way and for reporting after completion of the grant.

A portion of a worksheet for a year-long project might look like this:

Item	Description	Cost
Executive director	Supervision	10% of salary = $10,000 Benefits at 25% = $2,500
Project director	Hired in month one	11 months full time at $35,000 = $32,083
Tutors	12 working 10 hours per week for 13 weeks	12 x 10 x 13 x $4.50 = $7,020
Office space	Requires 25% of current space	25% x $20,000 = $5,000
Overhead	20% of project cost	20% x $64,628 = $12,926

With your worksheets in hand, you are ready to prepare the expense budget. For most projects, costs should be grouped into subcategories, selected to reflect the critical areas of expense. All significant costs should be broken out within the subcategories, but small ones can be combined on one line. You might divide your expense budget into personnel and nonpersonnel costs. Personnel subcategories might include salaries, benefits, and consultants. Subcategories under nonpersonnel costs might include travel, equipment, and printing, for example, with a dollar figure attached to each line.

Two expense budgets follow. The first example is from a proposal submitted by the YMCA of Eastern Union County to the Turrell Fund.

Personnel Expenses	
Salaries/Exempt	$ 42,999
Salaries/Program	31,245
Benefits—Health Care	2,328
Benefits—S.S.	5,654
Benefits—Unemployment & Disability	1,045
Subtotal	**$ 86,284**
Other Than Personnel Expenses	
Office Supplies	$ 250
Supplies Program	7,042
Field Trips	3,000
Supplies Program Food	5,000
Books	50
Equipment Program	2,300
Equipment—Computer	300
Advertising	350
Travel YMCA Vehicle	1,500
Conference Training	1,690
Hand 2 Hand	3,750
Professional Fees Other	9,625
Subtotal	**$ 34,857**
Total Expense	**$121,141**

The next budget is from the East Side House proposal to the Altman Foundation.

Exhibit A

EAST SIDE HOUSE
Mott Haven Village Preparatory High School
After School Enrichment and Supportive Services Budget

	2003–2004
EXPENSES	
After School Personnel	
Assistant Executive Director (10%)	$ 7,210
Deputy Director (20%)	8,240
Program Director	51,500
Social Worker	30,900
Educational Counselor (FT)	36,050
Educational Counselor (PT)	15,450
2 Tutors (PT)	25,750
Fringe Benefits (20%)	26,780
Subtotal After School Personnel	**$201,880**
After School Non-Personnel Expenses	
Recruitment/Outreach	$ 2,500
PSAT/SAT Prep	20,000
Educational Program Activities	18,000
Recreational Program Activities	5,000
Education, Career, Personal Development Workshops	15,000
Artists in Residence	25,000
Cultural Enrichment Activities	10,000
Family Building Activities	12,000
Technology Programming/Transportation	23,000
Computer Software	10,000
Staff Training/Development	25,000
Closing Ceremony/Student Awards	3,000
Subtotal After School Non-Personnel	**$166,000**
Grand Total of After School Activities	**$367,880**

Support and Revenue Statement

For the typical project, no support and revenue statement is necessary. The expense budget represents the amount of grant support required. But if grant support has already been awarded to the project, or if you expect project activities to generate income, a support and revenue statement is the place to provide this information.

In itemizing grant support, make note of any earmarked grants; this will suggest how new grants may be allocated. The total grant support already committed should then be deducted from the "Total Expenses" line on the expense budget to give you the "Amount to Be Raised" or the "Balance Requested."

Any earned income anticipated should be estimated on the support and revenue statement. For instance, if you expect 50 people to attend your performance on each of the four nights it is given at $10 a ticket, and if you hope that 20 of them will buy the $5 souvenir book each night, you would show two lines of income, "Ticket Sales" at $2,000 and "Souvenir Book Sales" at $400. As with the expense budget, you should keep backup worksheets for the support and revenue statement to remind yourself of the assumptions you have made.

Because an earned income statement deals with anticipated revenues, rather than grant commitments in hand, the difference between expenses and revenues is usually labeled "Balance Requested," rather than "Amount to Be Raised." The funder will appreciate your recognition that the project will earn even a small amount of money—and might well raise questions about this if you do not include it in your budget.

Now that your budget is complete, take the time to analyze it objectively. Be certain that the expense estimates are neither too lean nor on the high side. If you estimate too closely, you may not be able to operate within the budget. You will have to go back to funders already supporting the project for additional assistance, seek new donors, or underwrite part of the cost out of general operating funds. None of these alternatives is attractive.

Consistently overestimating costs can lead to other problems. The donor awards a grant expecting that all of the funds will support the project, and most will instruct you to return any funds remaining at the end. If you have a lot of money left over, it will reflect badly on your budgeting ability. This will affect the funder's receptiveness toward any future budgets you might present.

Finally, be realistic about the size of your project and its budget. You will probably be including a copy of the organization's financial statements in the appendix to your proposal. A red flag will be raised for the proposal reviewer if the budget for a new project rivals the size of the rest of your operation.

If you are inexperienced in developing proposal budgets, you should ask your treasurer or someone who has successfully managed grant funds to review it for you. This can help you spot obvious problems that need to be fixed, and it can prepare you to answer questions that proposal reviewers might raise, even if you decide not to change the budget.

Budget Narrative

A budget narrative portion is used to explain any unusual line items in the budget and is not always needed. If costs are straightforward and the numbers tell the story clearly, explanations are redundant.

If you decide a budget narrative is needed, you can structure it in one of two ways. You can create "Notes to the Budget," with footnote-style numbers on the line items in the budget keyed to numbered explanations. Or, if an extensive or more general explanation is required, you can structure the budget narrative as straight text. Remember, though, that the basic narrative about the project and your organization belong elsewhere in the proposal, not in the budget narrative.

The following is an example of a budget with an accompanying footnoted narrative from the Canal Community Alliance proposal.

Canal Community Alliance
Radio Canal Remote Studio Project Budget
As of April 4, 2003

Project Expenses	Amount Requested					
	CCA	Milagro Foundation	Marin Arts Council	The Bothin Foundation	Project Budget	Notes
Construction of office and studio space	$8,250				$ 8,250	a
Mixing Board				$ 4,000	4,000	b
MAC I Book				1,800	1,800	c
Pro-Tools Music Editing Software				1,500	1,500	d
Microphones		$ 250			250	e
Microphone stands		100	$150		250	f
Headphones			270		270	g
Speakers			80	20	100	h
1 Dual CD player		500			500	i
2 CART machines		1,200		1,750	2,950	j
Dedicated telephone line				550	550	k
Internet services for a year				200	200	l
Furniture				1,400	1,400	m
Carpet				1,500	1,500	n
Cables and wire adapters				400	400	o

Project Expenses	CCA	Milagro Foundation	Marin Arts Council	The Bothin Foundation	Project Budget	Notes
2 Wood doors with small window				650	650	p
Sound proofing material and installation		700		800	1,500	q
Curtains/drapes for windows				400	400	r
Radio Engineer @ $50/hr x 50 hours				2,500	2,500	s
Total Expenses	**$8,250**	**$2,750**	**$500**	**$17,470**	**$28,970**	

a. Remodeling and construction of office and studio space at CCA Teen Center.

b. Mixing board will be used to produce interviews and radio segments.

c. Laptop computer will be used in the production room which is a former closet and has no room for a desktop computer.

d. Music editing software for 3 computers @ $500 each

e. 5 mikes x $50 each

f. 5 mike stands x $50 each

g. 6 headphones @ $45 each

h. 4 speakers @ $25 each

i. CD player will be used to play music on the air.

j. Radio cart machines will be used to record and play PSAs, radio segments, and interviews. This includes one DLPS Cart-play @ $1,150 and one DLRS Cart-record @ $1,800.

k. Installation of a phone line for transmitting radio signal to and from San Rafael High School's transmitter.

l. Cost for DSL internet service for one year.

m. Furniture for meetings and production use. This includes a round table with chairs, 3 desk chairs, & a table for the mixing board.

n. The teen center does not have any carpet. Carpet is needed for Radio Canal's office and studio space.

o. Cables and wiring for installing equipment.

p. 2 Solid wood doors with a small window for production rooms; includes installation.

q. Sound proofing material and installation.

r. Curtains will be used as part of soundproofing on a wall with windows.

s. Technical consultant to select, wire and install all radio equipment

The budget, whether one page or several, is now ready to include in the proposal document. Keep a copy of it with your backup worksheets in a special folder. The materials in this folder will assist you in tracking actual expenses as the project unfolds. They will enable you to anticipate lines that are in danger of going over budget or areas where you might have extra funds to spend, so that you can manage effectively the grant funds that you receive. These materials will also be extremely helpful when it comes time to write the grant report. An example of a program budget will be found in the sample proposal in Appendix A.

7

Developing the Master Proposal: Organization Information and Conclusion

Organization Information

Normally the resume of your nonprofit organization should come at the end of your proposal. Your natural inclination may be to put this information up front in the document, but it is usually better first to sell the need for your project and *then* your agency's ability to carry it out.

It is not necessary to overwhelm the reader with facts about your organization. This information can be conveyed easily by attaching a brochure or other prepared statement or by providing brief information and then referring the funder to your organization's Web site, if you have one. In two pages or less, tell the reader when your nonprofit came into existence; state its mission, being certain to demonstrate how the subject of the proposal fits within or extends that mission; and describe the organization's structure, programs, and special staff expertise. The following example is from a proposal submitted to the Bella Vista Foundation by the Edgewood Center for Children and Families.

Organization history, mission, and types of programs provided

Edgewood Center for Children and Families was founded in 1851, as a refuge for orphans of the Gold Rush Era. For 152 years, Edgewood has provided a loving home for abused, neglected, and abandoned children. We are the oldest continually operating children's charity in the West.

In the 1980s, Edgewood began adding prevention and early intervention services as well. Our hope was to prevent children and families from ever needing our intensive residential care. Today, we serve 5,000 children and families each year with program sites in San Francisco, South San Francisco, East Palo Alto, and 25 public schools. Our four program areas are:

- *Kinship Support Network:* The Kinship Support Network serves families headed by grandparents, aunts, and uncles who have taken in a child as an alternative to foster care. Last year, we served 1,000 children and 600 caregivers in San Francisco and San Mateo Counties.

- *School-based services:* We provide child and family services on-site in the schools, ranging from after-school programs to family support to teacher training. Services are now placed in 25 SFUSD schools, reaching 2,800 children and families per year.

- *Residential treatment and school:* These programs serve abused and neglected children ages 6 to 14 whose severe emotional disturbances make it impossible for them to remain in their home, foster home, or neighborhood school. About 110 children are served each year.

- *Individualized services for children in crisis:* These services are targeted to children with severe emotional disturbances. If a child is facing a difficult crisis, Edgewood can provide one-on-one care to make sure the child does not have to leave his home or school.

Edgewood also provides technical assistance statewide and nationwide to help other organizations replicate our Kinship Support Network. Our San Mateo Kinship Support Network earned the 2002 "Friends of the Child Award" from the San Mateo Child Abuse Council.

Discuss the size of the board, how board members are recruited, and their level of participation. Give the reader a feel for the makeup of the board. (You should include the full board list in the appendix.) If your agency is composed of volunteers or has an active volunteer group, describe the functions that the volunteers fill. Provide details on the staff, including numbers of full- and part-time staff and their levels of expertise.

Describe the kinds of activities in which your staff engage. Explain briefly the assistance you provide. Describe the audiences you serve, any special or unusual needs they face, and why they rely on your agency. Cite the number of people who are reached through your programs.

Tying all of the information about your nonprofit together, cite your agency's expertise, especially as it relates to the subject of your proposal.

This information, coupled with the attachments you will supply in the appendix, is all the funder will require at this stage. Keep in mind that funders may wish to check with other sources to help evaluate your organization and its performance.

These sources might include experts in the field, contacts established at organizations similar to your own, other funders, or even an agency such as the BBB Wise Giving Alliance, which issues reports on some of the larger, national groups.

In the next sample, City Life/Vida Urbana briefly describes its history to the Hyams Foundation, Inc.

History and Mission

City Life/Vida Urbana is a bilingual grassroots community organization, established in 1973 in Jamaica Plain (JP) to organize and empower neighborhood residents. We are committed to fighting for racial, social, and economic justice by building the power of low-income and working-class people through four interrelated program areas: individual assistance and advocacy, education, coalition building, and direct action. Our fundamental organizing strategy is to develop the capacity of residents, particularly Latinos, women, and working-class people, to organize themselves and to take leadership in their own neighborhood. The fact that our bilingual, multicultural membership, Board, and staff closely mirror the resident population and actively address diversity challenges has helped make possible our many concrete victories, as well as progress toward community empowerment.

City Life/Vida Urbana's goal is to foster community activism and leadership development, particularly among low-income and immigrant residents. Over the past 29 years we have primarily focused on housing as the area through which we reach our goal. Housing is a critical issue for our members and has the power to utilize diverse community members to create a common agenda. We also organize around other issues that our community considers critical, such as workers' rights, youth empowerment, welfare "reform," and public school accountability. City Life is proof that local residents can, when active and organized, significantly improve their own lives.

Conclusion

Every proposal should have a concluding paragraph or two. This is a good place to call attention to the future, after the grant is completed. If appropriate, you should outline some of the follow-up activities that might be undertaken, to begin to prepare your funders for your next request.

This section is also the place to make a final appeal for your project. Briefly reiterate what your nonprofit wants to do and why it is important. Underscore why your agency needs funding to accomplish it. Don't be afraid at this stage to use a bit of emotion to solidify your case.

Two examples follow. The first is the conclusion to a proposal from Family Focus to the William Randolph Foundation. It is a strong restatement of the facts that appeared in the body of the proposal.

Conclusion

Family Focus is a leader in each of the communities it serves, helping participants build confidence in their own abilities. The programs that Family Focus offers link participants to crucial community resources in the Chicago metropolitan area and support children in the context of their families. The overall goals of Family Focus include: (1) improving the physical and emotional health of children, youth, and parents; (2) reducing social isolation and encouraging the development of social networks; (3) promoting positive parenting and strengthening the parent-child relationship; (4) increasing participants' educational attainment and their ability to advocate on behalf of themselves and their families; and (5) connecting families to additional community resources.

A $100,000 grant from the William Randolph Hearst Foundation will help Family Focus achieve its goals, which closely fit your goals of strengthening families and ensuring healthy child development, and promoting literacy. By supporting the general operating costs of Family Focus, the William Randolph Hearst Foundation will help build our capacity to support children and families as they face a variety of challenges. We hope you will partner with Family Focus to provide comprehensive family support services that help ensure children in the Chicago area have the best possible start in life.

The second example is from the YMCA of Eastern Union County proposal to the Turrell Fund.

Conclusion

Effective community youth organizations help youth beat the odds of early pregnancy, futures lost to drugs or academic failure.

The YMCA of Eastern Union County is where our local kids feel safe after school, evenings or on the weekends. It's where they participate in hundreds of far-reaching and wide-ranging programs that feature tutoring and academics, sports, mentoring, community service and life skills. And most important, it's where they can build the strength and confidence to make positive life choices.

The obstacles faced by today's teens are daunting. Much more than previous generations, they are faced with day-to-day choices that have true life and death ramifications. At the YMCA, we care deeply about the welfare and safety of our teens. We nurture them while engaging them in interesting, meaningful and useful activities.

To continue our services to these youth, the YMCA of Eastern Union County requests financial support from the Turrell Fund. A grant from the Turrell Fund would be an investment in the economically disadvantaged youth of the communities we serve. Your support would be an investment in their future.

8

Variations on the Master Proposal Format

In the preceding chapters we presented the recommended format for components of the standard proposal. In reality, however, not every proposal will slavishly adhere to these guidelines. This should not be surprising. Sometimes the scale of the project might suggest a small-scale letter format proposal, or the type of request might not require all of the proposal components or the components in the sequence recommended here. The guidelines and policies of individual funders will be your ultimate guide. Many funders today state that they prefer a brief letter proposal; others require that you complete an application form. In any case, you will want to refer to the basic proposal components (see Chapter 2) to be sure that you have not omitted an element that will support your case.

What follows is a description of a letter proposal and of other format variations.

A Letter Proposal

The scale of the project will often determine whether it requires a letter or the longer proposal format. For example, a request to purchase a $300 fax machine for your agency simply does not lend itself to a lengthy narrative. A small contribution to your agency's annual operating budget, particularly if it is a renewal of past support, might also warrant a letter rather than a full-scale proposal.

What are the elements of a letter request? For the most part, they should follow the format of a full proposal, except with regard to length. The letter should be no more than three pages. You will need to call upon your writing skills because it can be very hard to get all of the necessary details into a concise, well-articulated letter.

As to the flow of information, follow these steps while keeping in mind that you are writing a letter to someone. It should not be as formal in style as a longer proposal would be. It may be necessary to change the sequence of the text to achieve the correct tone and the right flow of information.

Here are the components of a good letter proposal, with excerpts of relevant sections of a letter proposal from NPower NY to the Hyde and Watson Foundation.

Ask for the gift: The letter should begin with a reference to your prior contact with the funder, if any. State why you are writing and how much funding is required from the particular foundation.

Dear Mr. Corbin:

On behalf of NPower NY, I am pleased to submit a proposal for consideration by the Hyde and Watson Foundation for $15,000 in support of NPower NY's workforce development program, Technology Service Corps (TSC).

Describe the need: In a very abbreviated manner, tell the funder why there is a need for this project, piece of equipment, etc.

The Need

In a set of focus groups held by NPower NY in summer 2000 and spring 2001, nonprofit professionals expressed frustration around the issue of IT staffing: their inability to recruit due to high salary expectations, their inability to retain staff due to lack of career opportunities, and their inability to stimulate innovative thinking beyond the usual repair and maintenance of PCs and networks. In the private sector, the ratio is usually one additional support person for every 50–75 computer users (assuming there is already other technology support—e.g., network administration, database administrator). However, nonprofits often work with zero or one technology administrator for as many as 100–150 staff. The TSC program is designed to help fill this important personnel gap.

Explain what you will do: Just as you would in a fuller proposal, provide enough detail to pique the funder's interest. Describe precisely what will take place as a result of the grant.

Technology Service Corps

The TSC program, which launched in January 2002, trains talented youth, age 18 to 25, from low-income communities in New York City on networking, computer basics and web development skills and then works with nonprofits to place them in available staff positions as junior information technology administrators. We selected this target population for several reasons: 1) to fulfill the need for nonprofit IT staff, 2) to create career-track job opportunities for New York City's young people, and 3) to groom the next generation of young people committed to a career in the nonprofit sector.

TSC candidates must meet baseline requirements that include: previous work experience, a high school diploma or GED, a desire for a career path in the technology field, and a keen interest in nonprofit work. The students are put through a

---

rigorous 12-week program that includes networking, computer basics, and web development skills training, and a 4-week internship in a nonprofit. All class modules include professional skills development, hands-on learning, and homework.

Since January 2002, we have held three classes as part of the TSC program with a total of 24 students admitted. The students represent the wealth of diversity that exists in New York City: 61 percent Hispanic, 30 percent African American, and 9 percent Asian American. The program is staffed by the TSC Associate and a part-time classroom instructor. To date, TSC has graduated 19 students—17 men and 2 women—and placed them in nonprofit jobs with salaries ranging from $22,000 to $26,000. TSC students also donated 400 hours of technology assistance to the nonprofit community.

The TSC program sets high standards and expectations for each one of its students and evaluates progress throughout the program. In 2003, success will be determined by running three cycles where students acquire advanced technology skills, 80 percent graduate, and 60 percent of graduates are placed in jobs.

Provide agency data: Help the funder know a bit more about your organization by including your mission statement, brief description of programs offered, number of people served, and staff, volunteer, and board data, if appropriate.

Background

NPower NY is a 501(c)(3) tax-exempt, nonprofit technology assistance provider dedicated to helping New York City nonprofits use information technology more effectively in serving their communities and accomplishing their missions. It launched in spring 2001 and currently has 167 nonprofit members. NPower NY offers a continuum of technology services including consulting, training, and membership support. NPower NY also operates an innovative workforce development program, Technology Service Corps, which trains talented New York City youth on networking, computer basics and web development skills and then works with nonprofits to place them in the nonprofit sector as junior information technology administrators. By offering hands-on help directly in communities, and partnering with others to bring appropriate online tools and resources, we are able to offer a continuum of affordable and accessible technology capacity building services to most nonprofit organizations—regardless of their size, resources or geographic location within the five boroughs of New York City. Our mission is to provide nonprofits with the technology tools and resources they need to further their missions and better serve their communities.

NPower NY is an affiliate of NPower, a Seattle-based nonprofit technology assistance provider. In partnership with the Microsoft Corporation, NPower is expanding its model to a dozen other cities across the United States over the next two years. NPower NY is the first affiliate to emerge out of the NPower-Microsoft partnership, and in less than two years has seen its budget grow to over $1.6 million in 2002 with a staff increase to 18 full-time employees and 4 part-time employees.

Include appropriate budget data: Even a letter request may have a budget that is a half page long. Decide if this information should be incorporated into the letter or in a separate attachment. Whichever course you choose, be sure to indicate the total cost of the project. Discuss future funding only if the absence of this information will raise questions.

Close: As with the longer proposal, a letter proposal needs a strong concluding statement.

A grant of $15,000 from the Hyde and Watson Foundation would enable the purchase of an LCD projector and 5 new laptops for the Technology Service Corps classroom, and home computers for students to continue refining their skills outside of class.

Thank you for your consideration of our request to support our workforce development program, Technology Service Corps. We look forward to offering brighter futures for talented, career- and community-minded youth in New York City. Please feel free to contact me or Lystra Batchoo, Development Associate, with any questions. We can be reached at 212-564-7010, ext. 208 or ext. 211 or by email at Barbara@NpowerNY.org or Lystra@NPowerNY.org.

Attach any additional information required: The funder may need much of the same information to back up a small request as a large one: a board list, a copy of your IRS determination letter, financial documentation, and brief resumes of key staff. Rather than preparing a separate appendix, you should list the attachments at the end of a letter proposal, following the signature.

It may take as much thought and data gathering to write a good letter request as it does to prepare a full proposal (and sometimes even more). Don't assume that because it is only a letter, it isn't a time-consuming and challenging task. Every document you put in front of a funder says something about your agency. Each step you take with a funder should build a relationship for the future.

Other Variations in Format

Just as the scale of the project will dictate whether a letter or a full proposal is indicated, so the type of request will be the determining factor as to whether all of the components of a full proposal are required.

The following section will explore the information that should appear in the proposal application for five different types of requests: special project, general purpose, capital, endowment, and purchase of equipment.

Special Project

The basic proposal format presented in earlier chapters uses the special project proposal as the prototype, because this is the type of proposal that you will most often be required to design. As stated previously, foundations tend to prefer to make grants for specific projects because such projects are finite and tangible, and their results are measurable. Most special project proposals will follow this format, or these basic components will be developed in a letter.

General Purpose

A general purpose proposal requests operating support for your agency. Therefore, it focuses more broadly on your organization, rather than on a specific project. All of the information in the standard proposal should be present, but there will not be a separate component describing your organization. That information will be the main thrust of the entire proposal. Also, your proposal budget will be the budget for the entire organization, so it need not be duplicated in the appendix.

Two components of the general purpose proposal deserve special attention. They are the need statement and program information, which replaces the "project description" component. The need section is especially important. You must make the case for your nonprofit organization itself, and you must do it succinctly. What are the circumstances that led to the creation of your agency? Are those circumstances still urgent today? Use language that involves the reader, but be logical in the presentation of supporting data. For example, a local organization should cite local statistics, not national ones.

The following is an example of a need statement from a general purpose proposal for Canal Community Alliance to the Bothin Foundation.

The Need for Community-Based, Culturally-Appropriate Services for Youth and Their Families

Recent immigrants and refugees face enormous obstacles and problems. Language and cultural barriers contribute to isolation, desperation, fear and anxiety. Access to services is limited, usually because most programs are unable to provide language and culturally appropriate assistance. Seeking assistance in an alien system and foreign language can be daunting, distressing and/or humiliating. Also, many recent immigrants fled countries where officials were to be feared or distrusted, and as a result, they are afraid to go to official sources for assistance. Canal families need a place where they can find information, emergency assistance, advocacy services and the resources to develop the skills to help them become self-sufficient and integrate into the broader community. They need assistance from staff like ours who are culturally competent, trusted by the community, and are easily accessible to everyone who comes though our door. Canal Community Alliance is that place.

While growing up in poverty and overcrowded housing conditions leads to a poorer quality of life, youth who live in non-English speaking or limited-English speaking households experience even greater barriers to academic and career attainment. Canal parents with non-English speaking or limited-English speaking ability are unable to help their children with their homework. Furthermore, because parents need to work two or three jobs in order to earn enough income to provide for their families, many Canal youth lack the necessary adult guidance and support to succeed in school. Although they are intelligent, perceptive and aware, they perform poorly and risk expulsion from school due to academic and behavioral programs. They are at risk of becoming school dropouts and engaging in destructive activities such as drug abuse and gang involvement.

Consider including details on recent accomplishments and future directions as seen in this excerpt from the Canal Community Alliance proposal.

Innovative Youth Training and Leadership Program

Canal Community Alliance's Youth Development and Leadership program (YDL) offers teens and pre-teens creative and healthy alternatives to destructive behavior through education, peer counseling, recreation, job skills training, life skills training, and leadership development. It also offers family support through case management, gang intervention, parent training, and community advocacy. YDL staff provide youth with the help, incentive and support they need to overcome the challenges of adolescence and become responsible and productive adults.

The Centerpiece of our YDL program is Radio Canal, an award winning youth radio project, which provides a vital voice for youth and the Spanish-speaking community. Radio Canal is directed and produced by student interns, community volunteers and staff. It was created to fill a need for a local media resource that provides culturally appropriate community information and education for the Latino community living in San Rafael and other areas of Marin. Radio Canal's slogan is "The Voice of Your Community" ("La Voz de Tu Comunidad"). Now in its fifth year, it reaches most of the diverse households in our neighborhood with a variety of programs. For example, last year we added a regular program in Mayan to reach more listeners. Radio Canal broadcasts three evenings a week from KSRH, on FM 88.1, the 10-watt station at San Rafael High School, and has a broadcast radius of 5 miles. We collaborate with the Marin County Office of Education and San Rafael High School to use the existing radio station at the high school. The weekly format includes Youth Canal News, public service announcements, job listings, Latino music, pre-recorded and live interviews, and

Youth Connection, a panel of teens discussing topics of special interests (i.e., teen health, cross-cultural awareness).

Providing Job Training, Life Skills and Leadership Opportunities
Radio Canal interns gain hands-on experience working at a radio station. Program interns and graduates are at-risk, bilingual students from Davidson Middle School, San Rafael and Terra Linda High Schools, and College of Marin. They receive training in all aspects of preparing and producing a radio program. Not only do interns develop skills in journalism, electronics, programming and music production, they also learn good work habits and attitude, punctuality and attendance, employee/employer relations, personal grooming and dress for the workplace, and how to keep a job. Interns are required to commit to at least one semester of radio training, attend weekly program planning sessions, and must complete a requisite number of on-air time hours. Weekly planning sessions emphasize team building and leadership skills. Currently, there are 11 middle school, high school and college students participating in Radio Canal. CCA staff, peer trainers and graduates of Radio Canal conduct the training sessions. Several of the students have stayed in the program 2–3 years taking advantage of continued trainings. Graduates of Radio Canal's internship program serve as mentors to the younger students.

Making Positive Changes in Young People's Lives
Producing the radio program helps at-risk youth develop basic job skills essential to employment, maintain or improve their bilingual linguistics, learn communication skills, and gain the self-confidence to succeed in life. Here are examples of how Radio Canal has made a positive impact on the lives of our interns:

- Elsa was one of the first students who helped plan the radio project. She stayed with Radio Canal for 2 years. After graduating from high school, she began volunteering with Wild 94.9FM in San Francisco. She now has a paying position at 94.9FM.

- Elena was very shy and soft spoken when she came to Radio Canal. As an on-air personality, she developed a booming, upbeat voice that helped her overcome some of the shyness. Today she is working extremely hard at the College of Marin to earn the grades she needs to achieve her ultimate goal of attending USC and studying communications.

- Gaby graduated from San Rafael High School last year and completed a semester at College of Marin. Using the skills she learned at Radio Canal, she started her own DJ business, called Aragon Entertainment, which provides DJ music at parties and quinceañeras. She also teaches the younger Radio Canal interns about mixing music and operating equipment.

- Edgar was a wiry 14-year-old who was involved in gang activities when he started with the radio. Radio Canal has helped him relax and stay off the streets. Today at 16, he is a sophomore at Terra Linda High School and has stayed away from fights and other street activities. Edgar produces and runs his own show with confidence.

- Marisol, 15, was not doing well in school, didn't like to do her homework and got into fights at school when she first came to Radio Canal about a year ago. Now, she is more interested in her schoolwork and she hasn't gotten into a fight in at least 6 months. As her self-esteem rose, she has become less timid and more outspoken on the microphone. She also has her own show, which she looks forward to and does enthusiastically.

Providing Culturally-Appropriate, Bilingual Community Education and Outreach

In addition to being an innovative youth training program, Radio Canal serves as vital resource for Marin's Spanish-speaking community who rely on Radio Canal for information about current events and local news. Through Radio Canal more than 25,000 people in the broadcast area have a chance to hear about the lives and accomplishments of their neighbors and be informed of what's happening around them. This helps them feel more connected and proud of the place where they live. The youth in the Canal neighborhood benefit because it gives them access to community radio, where they can participate in discussions on youth violence, relations with parents, college, and other subjects that impact their lives.

Radio Canal is also a viable tool for public agencies needing to outreach to Spanish-speaking residents. For example, Radio Canal staff and interns produced a live broadcast of San Rafael School District public hearings and produced bilingual public service announcements for the Marin County of Department of Health and Human Services, and Marin Employment Connection. In 2000, the Radio Canal team received the Marin Community Foundation's Neighborhood Achievement Award, which honors groups that make a positive difference in their communities. MCF President Tom Peters said, "We were just absolutely struck with the ingenuity and creativity of these students."

Capital

A capital proposal requests funds for facility purchase, construction, or renovation, or possibly land purchase or long-term physical plant improvements. Today many institutions include other items in a capital campaign, such as endowment funds, program expansion, and salaries for professors. But, for our purposes, we will discuss the more traditional definition of capital, that is, "bricks and mortar."

All of the components of a proposal will be included in a capital request. Differences in content will be found mainly in the need statement, the project description, the budget, and the appendix.

The need section in the capital proposal should focus on why the construction or renovation is required. The challenge is to make the programs that will use the facility come alive to the reader. For example, your agency may need to expand its day care program because of the tremendous need in your community among working parents for such support, the long waiting list you have, and the potential educational value to the children. Your proposal will be less compelling if the focus of the need statement is purely related to space considerations or to meeting building code requirements.

Following is an excerpt from a capital proposal for Ridgewood YMCA and the YMCA of Bergen County.

The Need:

The building at 112 Oak Street was dedicated in 1951 as the first jointly owned YMCA/YWCA facility ever built. A major addition in 1985 added a second swimming pool, a fitness facility and other program space. No major improvements or additions have been made since that time. Although the facility is maintained in a superior fashion with an emphasis on cleanliness, a 50+ year old building that gets constant use year-round needs a facelift and rejuvenation to keep pace with the advancements in programming requirements and an increased membership.

Recognizing the long-term planning implications of needs identified in the Ridgewood area, the YMCA and YWCA conducted a study to survey both active and former members, program staff and community leaders. A local architectural firm, Poskanzer-Skott Architects, was engaged to produce a Facilities Feasibility Study and Master Plan responding to the needs identified in this study.

This study indicated a strong need for a more modern facility, providing user-friendly, full access for all to program and administrative areas. Security and comfort are priorities in the architect's design, as well as complete compliance in all areas of the building with the Americans with Disabilities Act requirements. Traffic flow, outside for vehicular traffic and inside for our members and guests, will improve to insure an efficient delivery of programs and services with an emphasis on safety and convenience for all. Modern temperature control techniques and air-handling equipment will mean a truly year-round facility under all climatic conditions. Under present conditions, certain areas of the building cannot be used during extremely hot weather, and much of the building is not accessible to those with severe physical challenges.

All of the changes, additions and improvements included in this rejuvenation project are necessary for the YMCA and YWCA to meet the needs of its members today and in the future. As programs continue to grow in sophistication and new equipment makes exercise and rehabilitation more effective, the facility needs to change to accommodate this progress.

The project description component of a capital proposal includes two elements. The first is the description of how your programs will be enhanced or altered as a result of the physical work. Then should come a description of the physical work itself. The funder is being asked to pay for the latter and should have a complete narrative on the work to be undertaken. You might supplement that description with drawings, if available. These could be external views of the facility, as well as interior sketches showing people using the facility. Floor plans might help as well. These need not be formal renderings by an artist or an architect; a well-drawn diagram will often make the case. Photos showing "before" and drawings indicating what the "after" will be like are also dramatic adjuncts to the capital proposal.

The budget for a capital proposal will be a very detailed delineation of all costs related to the construction, renovation, etc. It should include the following:

- Actual brick-and-mortar expenses: These should be presented in some logical sequence related to the work being undertaken. For example, a renovation project might follow an area-by-area description, or a construction project might be presented chronologically. Don't forget to include expenses for such items as construction permits in this section.

- Other costs: Salaries, fees, and related expenses required to undertake the capital improvements. Be certain to include in your budget the projected costs of architects, lawyers, and public relations and fundraising professionals. Many capital proposal writers fail to adequately anticipate such "soft" costs.

- Contingency: Estimates for actual construction costs often change during the fundraising and preconstruction periods. It is therefore a good idea to build a contingency into the budget in case costs exceed the budgeted amounts. A contingency of 10 to 20 percent is the norm; more than that tends to raise a proposal reviewer's eyebrows.

Here is the capital campaign budget for Ridgewood YMCA and YMCA of Bergen County project.

The Project Elements

New Entry, Renovations, Safety and Security Upgrades   **$1,750,000**

New lobby and orientation of building entry toward the North Parking Lot making the building more accessible from the member's parking area.

Upgrade, re-orient the reception, information and control desk area.

Added program space on the second floor.

Additional basement storage.

Retrofit first floor offices and lounge.

Renovate Child Care Center.

Add a central locker/control desk for all gymnasium and pool area activities.

Additional parking spaces in the North Parking Area.

Americans with Disabilities Act (ADA) Upgrades   **$ 450,000**

Handicap accessible elevator.

Changes on the second floor and basement to accommodate wheelchairs.

Other necessary improvements.

Heating, Ventilation (HVAC) and Electrical   **$1,250,000**

Upgrade ceiling and other lighting throughout building.

New HVAC system throughout building, adding much needed air conditioning to programming space for summertime use.

Code compliant electrical and fire safety system.

Upgrade air handling system in Grannon Pool.

Professional Fees (including Architectural, Legal, and Fundraising)   **$ 550,000**

Total Estimated Cost   **$4,000,000**

The appendix to a capital proposal may be expanded to include floor plans and renderings if they do not appear within the proposal text. If a brochure has been developed in conjunction with the capital campaign, this could be sent along as part of the appendix package.

Endowment

An endowment is used by nonprofits to provide financial stability and to supplement grant and earned income. Often campaigns, designed like capital drives, are mounted to attract endowment dollars. A proposal specifically requesting funding for endowment may resemble either a special project or a general operating application, depending on whether the endowment is for a special purpose, such as scholarships or faculty salaries, or for the organization's general operations. Your focus will be on the following components: the need statement, the program description, and the budget.

The need statement for an endowment proposal will highlight why the organization must establish or add to its endowment. Points to raise might include:

- the importance of having available the interest from the endowment's corpus as an adjunct to the operating budget;
- the desire to stabilize annual income, which is currently subject to the vagaries of government or other grants;
- the value of endowing a particular activity of your organization that lacks the capacity to earn income or attract gift support.

The project description will cover the impact of endowment dollars on the programs of your nonprofit. Provide as many details as possible in explaining the direct consequences of these dollars. Indicate if there are naming or memorial opportunities as part of the endowment fund.

The budget will round out all of this data by indicating how much you are trying to raise and in what categories. For example, there might be a need to endow 75 scholarships at $10,000 each for a total of $750,000.

Equipment

Frequently, organizations have a need to develop a free-standing proposal for purchase of a piece of equipment, be it MRI equipment for a hospital or a personal computer for program staff. These would require only a letter proposal, but the scale or significance of the purchase may dictate a full proposal. Again, the need statement, the project description, and the budget will be primary.

In the need statement, explain why the organization must have this equipment. For example, this hospital has no MRI equipment, and people in the community have to travel great distances when an MRI test is required.

Then in the project description, explain how the equipment will alter the way services are delivered. For example: "The new MRI equipment will serve some 500 people annually. It will assist in diagnoses ranging from structural problems in the foot to tracking the development of a lung tumor. The cost per procedure will be $1,000, but it will save millions in unnecessary surgical procedures."

This budget may be the easiest you will ever have to prepare. Indicate the purchase cost for the equipment, plus transportation and installation charges. Consider whether staff training to utilize the equipment properly and the added expenses of maintenance contracts should be included in your budget with the cost of its purchase.

9

Packaging the Proposal

Writing a well-articulated proposal represents the bulk of the effort in preparing a solid proposal package. The remaining work is to package the document for the particular funder to whom it is being sent, based on your research and your contact with that funder to date (as described in Chapters 10 and 11).

Be sure to check the foundation's instructions for how and when to apply. Some foundations will accept proposals at any time. Others have specific deadlines. Foundations will also differ in the materials they want a grant applicant to submit. Some will list the specific information they want and the format you should adopt. Others will have an application form. In the course of the interviews for this book, it became apparent that an increasing number of foundations are developing an application form or a specific proposal format as a means of helping consideration of diverse information in a concise and consistent manner. Many are posting these guidelines on their

Web sites. Whatever the foundation's guidelines, pay careful attention to them and follow them.

Grantmakers are extremely frustrated with applicants who do not take the time to find out what is in their application guidelines and then provide that information. It is in the grantseeker's best interest to follow the grantmaker's advice. Otherwise there are delays in reviewing the application while the grantmaker waits for the missing items. Foundation and corporate giving representatives express dismay at having review of worthy proposals delayed sometimes for up to a year because of requested items that are not included.

Of equal concern to grantmakers is the submission of attachments that are not required by the guidelines. Nonprofit applicants would be well advised to refrain from adding any unnecessary attachments—ever! Rather, interesting items not included in the proposal package might be sent to the prospect as part of good cultivation later on.

In the following pages we will discuss the packaging of the document, including:

- cover letter or letter of transmittal;
- cover and title pages;
- table of contents; and
- appendix.

The Cover Letter

Often the cover letter is the basis for either consideration or rejection. Hildy Simmons, formerly of J. P. Morgan Private Bank, states, "The cover letter is key. It should be clear and concise and make me want to turn the page. Here are a few dos and don'ts:

- Do make a specific request. It's inconvenient if we have to dig for it.
- Do include a couple of paragraphs about why you are applying to us. But don't quote back to us our own contribution report.
- Do note references but don't name drop."

Elizabeth Smith of the Hyams Foundation tells us, "The cover letter is the first thing that I read." Christine Park of Lucent

Technologies Foundation provides this recommendation: "Make your case quickly in the cover letter; provide the detail in the proposal." Maria Mottola of the New York Foundation notes: "This section makes a difference. We learn who wants this project to happen. It tells the story of the why and the how."

What a waste of your agency's resources to invest time, energy, and money developing a proposal around a terrific project and then not have it read! To avoid this happening, be clear, be succinct, and state immediately why the project fits within the funder's guidelines. For example, you might state, "Our funding research indicates that the XYZ Foundation has a special interest in the needs of children in foster care, which is the focus of this proposal." If the proposal does not fit the foundation's guidelines, this should be acknowledged immediately in the cover letter. You will then need to provide an explanation for why you are approaching this foundation.

If you had a conversation with someone in the funder's office prior to submitting the proposal, the cover letter should refer to it. For example, you might say, "I appreciate the time Jane Doe of your staff took to speak with me on December 1 about the Foundation." But do *not* imply that a proposal was requested if in fact it was not.

Sometimes in a discussion with a funder you will be told, "I can't encourage you to submit because. . . . However, if you want, you can go ahead and submit anyway." In this case, you should still refer to the conversation, but your letter should demonstrate that you heard what the funder said. To quote Mary Beth Salerno of the American Express Foundation, "It is smart to make this connection. As a matter of fact, it is a mistake not to mention it!"

The cover letter should also indicate what the reader will find in the proposal package. For example: "You will find enclosed two documents for your review. The first is a concise description of our project. The second is an appendix with the documents required by the Foundation for further review of our request."

Cite the name of the project, a précis of what it will accomplish, and the dollar amount of the request. For example: "Our After School Recreational Program will meet the educational and recreational needs of 50 disadvantaged Harlem children. We are seeking a grant of $25,000 from the Foundation to launch this project."

In the concluding paragraph of the cover letter, you should request a meeting with the funder. This can take place at the funder's office or on site at your agency. Also indicate your willingness to answer any questions that might arise or to provide additional information as required by the funder.

In summary, the cover letter should:

- indicate the size of the request;
- state why you are approaching this funder;
- mention any prior discussion of the proposal;
- describe the contents of the proposal package;
- briefly explain the project; and
- offer to set up a meeting and to provide additional information.

Who should sign the letter? Either the chairman of the board or the chief executive officer of your agency should be the spokesperson for all proposal submissions. Some funders insist on signature by the chairman of the board, indicating that the proposal has the support and endorsement of the board. However, signature by the executive director may allow for a sense of continuity that a rotating board chair cannot provide. If your group has no full-time staff, then the issue is resolved for you, and the board chairman should sign all requests. This would hold true also if your agency is in the process of searching for a new chief executive.

The proposal cover letter should never be signed by a member of the development staff. These individuals do the research, develop the proposals, and communicate with the funder, but generally they stay in the background when it comes to the submission of the proposal and any meetings with the funder. The individual who signs the cover letter should be the same person who signs subsequent correspondence, so that the organization has one spokesperson.

Variations may occur under special circumstances. For example, if a board member other than the chairperson is directly soliciting a peer, the cover letter should come from him or her. Alternatives would be for the letter to be signed by the chairman of the board and then for the board member to write a personal note on the original letter, or to send along a separate letter endorsing the proposal.

Following is a cover letter to the Hyde and Watson Foundation from Mount Saint Mary Academy. Note that the letter includes:

- reference to prior support;
- the request;
- information about the project and the organization; and
- a promise to supply additional information, if needed.

April 30, 2003
Mr. Hunter W. Corbin, President
The Hyde and Watson Foundation
437 Southern Boulevard
Chatham, NJ 07928

Dear Mr. Corbin:

We are grateful to you and the Trustees of The Hyde and Watson Foundation for your past efforts on behalf of Mount Saint Mary Academy and for providing a source of support for the mission of the school, its future and the future of all who embody the Mount community.

As you know, over the past year and a half we have been involved in the *Continuing the Mercy Legacy of Excellence Campaign,* which The Hyde and Watson Foundation so generously supported. This is a 4.2 million dollar, 26,000 sq. foot renovation and upgrading of our math and science areas, classrooms, student center/cafeteria, student activity areas and installation of fire suppression systems.

We have raised 3.3 million of the needed 4.2 million. We now have an opportunity to raise the balance through a challenge gift to Mount Saint Mary Academy.

In April 2002, an alumna and her husband pledged a challenge gift of $500,000. The family agreed to contribute a dollar for each two matching dollars. Mount Saint Mary Academy has raised $600,000 of the million dollars necessary to maximize the challenge gift. A current parent has pledged $200,000 toward this challenge, the largest pledge in our history.

It is because of The Hyde and Watson Foundation's generosity that I again approach you to consider a request for additional funds to help us maximize the Challenge Gift. A grant request for $50,000 and supporting materials are enclosed.

Thank you for your consideration to our request. We truly appreciate your support and I look forward to hearing from you. If you need more information or would prefer me to meet with you in person, please call.

May God continue to bless The Hyde and Watson Foundation and all its wonderful work.

Sincerely in Mercy,

S. Lisa D. Gambacorto, RSM, Ed. S.
Directress

Here is another example of a cover letter, this one from the Cora Hartshorn Arboretum and Bird Sanctuary to the E. J. Grassmann Trust. It has the following characteristics:

- It is brief.
- It requests specific support.
- It makes reference to actual and potential donors.
- It invites the grantmaker to make a site visit.

October 14, 2002

Mr. William V. Engel
Executive Director
E. J. Grassmann Trust
P. O. Box 4470
Warren, NJ 07059-0470

Dear Mr. Engel:

On behalf of the Cora Hartshorn Arboretum and Bird Sanctuary I am pleased to be in contact with you. I am writing to request support of the E. J. Grassmann Trust through a $25,000 grant toward *Campaign For Our Future.*

The Cora Hartshorn Arboretum and Bird Sanctuary is a non-profit organization serving as an environmental education and cultural center for the residents of greater Milburn Township and Essex Country. The Arboretum receives 17,500 visitors annually and is home to 45 species of trees, 150 species of wildflowers, and 100 species of birds. It is truly an oasis in the middle of suburbia.

If the Arboretum is to respond to the increased environmental education demands of the community while maintaining and enhancing the woodlands and trails, funds must be found. Specifically, the Arboretum must raise $3,000,000 to preserve the woodlands, enhance the educational programs and build the endowment.

Of that amount, more than $650,000 has already been raised from individuals, corporations, and foundations. Donors include one government source, the ___ Foundation and the ___ Foundation. This total includes a challenge grant from a generous individual who has pledged 10% of the total amount raised, which we currently estimate at $300,000. Several local organizations have also given to the campaign. In addition, we currently have pending proposals with foundations and corporations including the ___ Foundation and the ___ Foundation.

We have completed soliciting the Arboretum's Board and are pleased to report 100% participation and total gifts of $47,000. In addition to making their own gifts our 18 vice-chairs are currently soliciting major gifts from the community.

I have included a proposal outlining our goals for the campaign for your review. I would also be pleased to show you our facilities and grounds at any time. If you should have any questions or require any additional information please do not hesitate to contact me.

Thank you for your thoughtful consideration of this request. I look forward to hearing from you.

Sincerely,

Bonnie Chase
Executive Director

A final example is from the YWCA of Plainfield/North Plainfield, New Jersey. It was well received by the grantmaker who was familiar with the applying organization. Sometimes candor—mixed with a touch of self-effacing humor—can be very effective.

Mr. Robert Parsons, Jr.
Chairman
Charles E. & Joy C. Pettinos Foundation
437 Southern Boulevard
Chatham Township, NJ 07928

Dear Mr. Parsons:

I know, I know that my proposal is being submitted to you after March 1st. This is completely my fault, and I will understand if the foundation's managers determine that our request is ineligible for consideration at this time.

We have just entered into a new phase of the Campaign, and I have taken on a number of new responsibilities—and one of them was to submit this proposal. But I just didn't get up to speed in time.

If you are able to consider support for the YWCA, we will all be grateful. This is a big project for us, but it is going very well and we have experienced such kindness and generosity from so many in the past year.

Mr. Parsons, I appreciate your past support. If you are not able to accept this proposal now, I hope I will have the opportunity to resubmit at another time. But please don't report me to my Board!

Thank you again.

Sincerely,

Jacquelyn M. Glock, MSW
Executive Director

Cover Page and Title

The cover page has three functions:

1. to convey specific information to the reader;
2. to protect the proposal; and
3. to reflect the professionalism of the preparer.

You should personalize the information on the cover page by including the name of the funder. You might present the information as follows:

> A PROPOSAL TO THE XYZ FOUNDATION

or

> A REQUEST DEVELOPED FOR THE XYZ FOUNDATION

Then note the title of the project:

> A CAMPAIGN FOR STABILITY

Provide key information that the funder might need to contact your agency:

> Submitted by:
> The Nonprofit Organization
> 40 Canal Street
> New York, NY 10013
>
> | | |
> |---|---|
> | Mary Smith | Susan Jones |
> | Executive Director | Director of Development |
> | 212-935-5300 x23 | 212-935-5300 x21 |
> | 212-935-9660 (fax) | 212-935-9660 (fax) |
> | e-mail: MSmith@aol.com | e-mail: SJones@aol.com |

It is possible that your cover letter will be separated from the rest of the proposal once it arrives at its destination. Without key information on the cover page, the funder could fail to follow up with your agency. You are being kind to your prospective funder when you remember to add the following:

- phone extension or direct telephone line for both the person who signed the letter and a primary staff contact;
- fax number for your organization; and
- e-mail addresses for both the signer and staff contact, if available, since it is becoming increasingly common for funding representatives to contact you via e-mail with questions and requests for additional documentation.

The cover page from the East Side House proposal serves as an example.

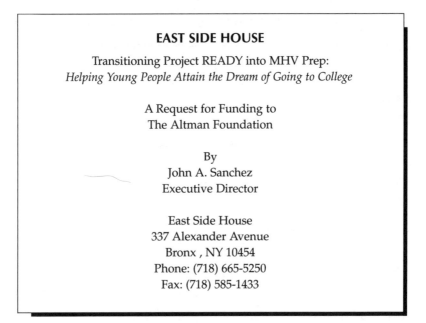

EAST SIDE HOUSE

Transitioning Project READY into MHV Prep:
Helping Young People Attain the Dream of Going to College

A Request for Funding to
The Altman Foundation

By
John A. Sanchez
Executive Director

East Side House
337 Alexander Avenue
Bronx , NY 10454
Phone: (718) 665-5250
Fax: (718) 585-1433

The title you assign to your proposal can have a surprisingly significant impact on the reader. It should reflect what your project is all about. "A CAMPAIGN FOR STABILITY" tells the reader that there is a formal effort taking place and that the result will be to bring stability to the nonprofit applicant. It is short and to the point, while being descriptive.

There are a few suggestions for developing the title for a proposal:

- Don't try to be cute. Fundraising is a serious matter. A cute title implies that the proposal is not a serious attempt to solve a real problem.
- Do not duplicate the title of another project in your agency or one of another nonprofit that might be well-known to the funder. It can cause confusion.
- Be sure the title means something. If it is just words, try again, or don't use any title at all.

Coming up with the title can be a tricky part of proposal writing. If you are stuck, try these suggestions:

- Seek the advice of the executive director, the project director, or a creative person in the organization or outside.
- Hold an informal competition among staff and/or volunteers to see who can come up with the best title.
- Go to the board with a few ideas and ask board members to select the one that makes the most sense.
- Jot down a list of key words from the proposal. Add a verb or two and experiment with the word order.

Let's take a look at a few actual titles and evaluate their effectiveness.

Title	Effectiveness
Forward Face	Arouses interest but does not tell you anything about the project.
	This is a proposal that seeks funds for facial reconstruction for disfigured children. With the help of the nonprofit group involved, the children will have a new image with which to face the future. The title is a pun, which is cute but not very effective.

Title	Effectiveness
Vocational, Educational Employment Project	This title tells us that three types of services will be offered.
	The project serves disadvantaged youth, which is not mentioned. The effectiveness of this title could be improved if the population served were somehow alluded to.
Building a Healthier Tomorrow	This title implies that construction will occur, and indeed it is the title for a capital campaign. It also suggests that the construction is for some kind of health facility.
	This proposal is for a YMCA to improve its health-wellness facilities. Thus, the title is very effective in conveying the purpose of the proposal.

You should evaluate any titles you come up with by anticipating the reaction of the uninitiated funding representative who will be reading this proposal.

Table of Contents

Obviously, for letter proposals or those of five pages or less, a table of contents is not required. For proposals of ten pages or more, a table of contents is essential.

Simply put, the table of contents tells the reader what information will be found in the proposal. The various sections should be listed in the order in which they appear, with page numbers indicating where in the document they can be located. The table should be laid out in such a way that it takes up one full page.

Following the proposal format we have recommended, a table of contents would look like this:

TABLE OF CONTENTS	Page
Executive Summary	1
Statement of Need	2
Project Description	4
Budget	7
Organization Information	9
Conclusion	10

By stating where to find specific pieces of information, you are being considerate of the proposal reader, who might want an overview of what information is included and also might want to be selective in the initial review.

A sample follows. It is from a proposal for Heads Up.

Table of Contents

   - IRS 501(c)(3) Letter of Determination
   - Key Staff Profiles
   - Board of Directors
   - Letters of Support
   - Additional Promotional Materials

The Appendix

The appendix is a reference tool for the funder. Include in it any information not included elsewhere that the foundation or corporate grantmaker indicates is required for review of your request. Not every proposal requires an appendix.

The appendix should be stapled together separately from the proposal narrative. Because it usually contains information that the funder has specifically requested, keeping it separate makes it easy for the funder to find those items. The appendix may have its own table of contents indicating to the reader what follows and where to find it.

A sample table of contents to a proposal appendix, taken from the Cora Hartshorn Arboretum and Bird Sanctuary proposal, follows:

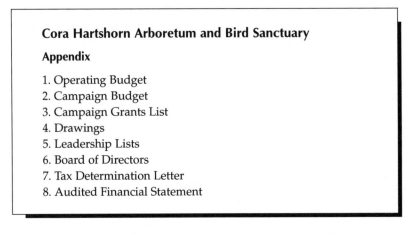

Cora Hartshorn Arboretum and Bird Sanctuary

Appendix

1. Operating Budget
2. Campaign Budget
3. Campaign Grants List
4. Drawings
5. Leadership Lists
6. Board of Directors
7. Tax Determination Letter
8. Audited Financial Statement

You may wish to include any or all of the following items in the appendix:

1. A board list. This should contain the name of each board member and that person's business or other affiliation. Adding further contact information such as address and telephone number is optional. The reader will use this to identify people he or she knows or whose names are familiar.

An excerpt from the board list for YMCA of Eastern Union County serves as an example:

YMCA of Eastern Union County
2002–2003 BOARD OF DIRECTORS

President:	James Masterson	Union Hospital
Vice President:	David Gibbons	David O. Evans, Inc.
Vice President:	James Steinruck	Elizabethtown Water Company
Treasurer:	Kevin McCloskey	Synergy Federal Savings Bank
Assistant Treasurer:	Belarmino Suarez	Mendonca & Suarez
Secretary:	Rod Spearman	Elizabethport Presbyterian Center
Members:	Martha DeNoble	Trinitas Hospital
	John Forrester	Summit Insurance Advisors
	Juan Grana, D. C.	Work Safe Enterprises
	John Jacobson	Jacobson & Company
	Jeffrey Jotz	City of Rahway
	Philip Krevsky, Esq.	Krevsky, Silber, Brown & Bergen
	Charles Minton	Minton's Fire and Security Specialists
	Alex Murray	A. J. Murray Associates
	Ann Revaitis	The Rahway Savings Institution
	Alexis Roiter, PhD	Consultant
	Raphael Salermo	Tri-State Home Furnishings
	Calvin Sierra	Imperial Weld Ring
	Maureen Tinen	Union County Economic Development Corporation

---

2. Your nonprofit's IRS Letter of Determination. This document, issued by the IRS, indicates that your agency has been granted 501(c)(3) status and is "not a private foundation." Gifts made to your organization are deductible for tax purposes. This letter is usually requested by funders. Foundations can give most easily to publicly supported organizations, and corporations want their gifts to be tax deductible. If your organization is religiously affiliated or a government entity, you might not have such a letter, and you should explain that fact to the funder.

3. Financial information. The operating budget for the current fiscal year and the latest audited financial statement are often appropriate to include. Some funders request your latest 990 in order to assess the financial stability of your organization. If your agency is religiously affiliated, or if for some other reason you do not file a 990, you will need to explain this fact to a funder that requests it. You may want to include a list of donors for the past fiscal year by name and size of gift. Grantmakers also want to know which foundations and corporations currently are being approached to help with the project under review, as well as who has already funded the project. An excerpt from the Booker T. Washington Learning Center's support list follows.

The East Harlem Urban Center
Booker T. Washington Learning Center
2002–2003 Grants List

Foundation/Corporation

Annie Eaton Society	$ 12,500
Lily Auchincloss Foundation	10,000
Carole A. and Norman Barham Foundation	5,000
Barker Welfare	7,500
Arthur Blank Family Foundation	25,000
Robert Bowne Foundation	20,000
Brick Church	11,000
Brick Church—Women's Assoc.	1,750
Louis Calder Foundation	15,000
Clark Foundation	25,000
Colgate Palmolive	3,000
Congregational Church of Manhasset	1,000
Dover Corporation	50,000
Dover Industries	2,400
Lily Palmer Fry Memorial Fund	2,500
Garden City Comm. Church	2,000
Greentree Foundation	10,000
Heart and Soul Charitable Fund	32,650
Heckscher Foundation for Children	10,000
Int'l Assoc. of Admin. Professionals	2,500
J. P. Morgan Chase Manhattan Foundation	2,500
JST Foundation	100
Little River Foundation	30,000
Madison Avenue Presbyterian	6,000
Metzger-Price Fund	2,000
New York Mercantile Exchange Foundation	10,000
Ohrstrom Foundation	2,500
Plymouth Church of Pilgrims	2,500
Santreece Foundation	30,000
St. James Church	5,000
Wantagh Memorial Church	200
Total	**$339,600**

The Learning Center's fiscal year runs from April 1st to March 31st.

4. Resumes of key staff. If the background information on key staff members is not included as part of the project statement of the proposal, it should be included in the appendix. This also might be the place to include the organization chart, if you feel it would be helpful.

Do not include in the appendix anything that is not required by the funder or deemed essential to making your case. The key is to give the funder what is needed for review of your proposal without making the package look overwhelming. For example, many nonprofits like to add press clippings to the appendix. If they make the package appear unnecessarily bulky and are tangential to the grant review, they should be sent to the funder at another time when they will receive more attention. However, should these clippings be essential to the review of the request, then by all means include them.

At this stage of assembling the proposal, you have a cover letter and two additional separately packaged components: the proposal narrative and the appendix. If each is clearly identifiable, you will save the funder time and energy in the initial review of your proposal.

Packaging

Packaging refers to both the physical preparation of the documents and their assembly.

Physical Preparation

Every proposal package should be individually prepared for each funder. This permits you to customize the submission in order to reflect the interests of a specific funder and to show them that you've done your homework. This is the point at which you need to double-check the guidelines for a funder's specific requirements for the proposal package.

With today's word-processing software, it will be relatively easy to customize the cover letter, title page, and other components of the package that have variables in them. For those components that are photocopied, be sure that the originals you are working from are crisp and legible. For example, if your IRS Letter of Determination is in poor condition, write to the Internal Revenue Service at I.R.S., TE/

GE, Room 4010, P.O. Box 2508, Cincinnati, OH 45201 (or call toll-free 1-877-829-5500), and ask for a fresh copy of the letter. The request must be on your organization's official letterhead. The letter should contain your organization's name, address, taxpayer ID number, and a daytime telephone number, and it must be signed by an officer with that person's title. For the other documents, copy from originals whenever possible.

Assembly

When a proposal arrives in a funder's office, any binding is usually removed before the proposal is reviewed. Therefore, do not waste money on binding for the proposal and the appendix. Simply staple each document, or use a plastic strip to hold together each document. Ruth Shack of Dade Community Foundation says, "No gloss, no covers. Do not spend money or time on elaborate presentations."

You have three documents: the cover letter, the proposal, and the appendix. The latter two are separately stapled. In all likelihood, these documents will require a manila envelope. Be certain that the addressee and return address information are printed clearly on the envelope. You might want to put a piece of cardboard in the envelope to protect the documents. Then insert the three documents with the cover letter on top, followed by the proposal and the appendix.

With regard to the funder's address, if you are following the procedure recommended in Chapter 11 for submitting this request, you will have had a conversation with the funder's office prior to submitting the proposal. Use that opportunity to verify the address and the name of the person to whom the package is to be sent.

Of course, the prior advice assumes you will be mailing in a proposal to a funder. Many of the grantmakers interviewed for this book indicate that they now accept proposals as documents attached to e-mail cover letters. Others say they expect to do so in the very near future. Still others are considering online application forms that grantseekers fill out and submit electronically. As E. Belvin Williams of the Turrell Fund explains, "We are exploring how to handle electronic proposals. What information will we sacrifice? We want to reduce the hard copy stuff and be more paper free." In many instances, however, the attachments such as the IRS designation letter, audited financials, and the organization's Form 990 still need to be mailed separately.

The grantmakers we interviewed suggest a few tips for those transmitting proposals electronically. First, don't wait until the last minute to submit the proposal just because you no longer need to rely on the U.S. mail. Second, be sure the document gets to the correct person. You can verify receipt by sending a follow-up e-mail query after the document was sent or by calling to be sure it was received. Third, don't send "broadcast" proposals by e-mail since they will receive no more serious consideration than mass mailings did in the past.

10

Researching Potential Funders

Once you have drafted your proposal, you are ready to develop your prospect list of foundations and/or corporations that might be interested in funding it. What you learn during this process will help you prepare different proposal packages, as described in Chapter 9, depending on the specific funder information you uncover.

The foundation and corporate executives interviewed for this book repeatedly advised grantseekers to pay special attention to the research effort. Most felt that sufficient information is available to enable nonprofit organizations to do their homework, thereby obtaining a clear picture of the interests of potential funders. As William Engel of the E.J. Grassmann Trust says, "Do your homework before you even make a call. The resources are out there. Use them." Laura Gilbertson of the William Bingham Foundation adds, "Cast as wide a net as possible."

There are three steps you should follow in conducting your research:

- Compile;
- Investigate;
- Refine.

Compile

Your ultimate goal is to compile a list of foundations, corporations, and other funders whose geographic and/or program interests might lead them to support your agency and the specific projects for which you are seeking funding. Try to be inclusive at this stage. If you think a specific foundation or corporate donor should be on the list, go ahead and include it. Let further research you conduct on that funder tell you otherwise.

At the compilation stage, you have a variety of resources to draw upon in addition to the standard print or online funding directories. Check your local newspaper for articles about corporations or businesses in your area. Talk to your local chamber of commerce and civic groups such as the Rotary and Lions Club. And, of course, utilize various search engines on the Internet. A foundation's Web site is often the best source for current guidelines and recent grants awarded. Be resourceful as you compile your list of possible funders.

You will also want to become aware of who is funding other agencies in your community. These foundations and corporations may be likely sources of support for your own agency as well. This information can be difficult to unearth. Sometimes another local agency's annual report or Web site will list its donors; nonprofits occasionally will publicly thank their funders in the local newspaper; arts organizations usually will list their donors in event programs. The grants database in *The Foundation Directory Online Plus, Premium,* and *Platinum; FC Search: The Foundation Center's Database on CD-ROM,* and the Foundation Center's *The Foundation Grants Index* on CD-ROM contain the names of recipients of grants from the nation's larger foundations.

Investigate

Next, take your list and investigate each source. There are definitive resources available to you to research foundations. The IRS requires private foundations to file an annual 990-PF form reporting on assets and grants. You will base your research on online and print directories that have been compiled using the 990-PF or from information provided directly to the directory publisher, on materials issued by the foundations themselves or on the 990-PF itself. It is more difficult to obtain information on corporate giving. As noted elsewhere, corporations may use two grantmaking vehicles: a private foundation and a corporate giving program. If a corporation has a foundation, then a 990-PF will be available, just as with other private foundations. If the corporation has a separate giving program, it is not required to file a publicly available report on gifts made under this program. Some corporations do issue special reports on their philanthropic endeavors, and a number of directories devoted specifically to corporate giving are published regularly. Corporate Web sites can also yield useful information on company philanthropic endeavors, if you know where to look.

Here is what you are looking for in any of the resources you use:

- A track record of giving in your geographic locale, in your field of interest, and for the type of support you seek, be it basic operating support, seed money, or funding for construction or equipment.
- Grants of a size compatible with your agency's needs. (Bear in mind that in all likelihood your project will have more than one funder.)
- Funders that have not already committed their resources many years into the future and that do not appear simply to fund the same nonprofit groups year in and year out.

Print and Electronic Directories

Appendix C contains a description of electronic and print resources you can utilize in your research. The Foundation Center is the pre-eminent source of information on foundation and corporate funders. *The Foundation Directory Online, FC Search: The Foundation Center's Database on CD-ROM*, the Center's print directories, and many other resources are made available to the public at its five libraries and more than 230 Cooperating Collections in sites across the country. The Center's collections also include copies of annual reports, press releases, historical materials, and articles on local or national foundations. Where detailed database or annual report information is lacking, you can examine copies of a foundation's 990-PF via Foundation Finder or the 990-PF Search feature at the Center's Web site (www.fdncenter.org) and in addition, via direct links from search results in *The Foundation Directory Online,* a family of searchable databases, available in a range of monthly and annual subscription options, or in *FC Search: The Foundation Center's Database on CD-ROM.*

Online databases, print and CD-ROM directories will most likely be your primary resource in investigating the foundations on your list. But you must not stop there. Often you will find additional or more up-to-date information in other resources, such as online subscription services and various Web sites.

The Internet

Grantseekers today are discovering a wealth of information on the Internet. Although locating that information can be daunting at first, there are many helpful resources on the subject. The Foundation Center maintains its own content-rich Web site, www.fdncenter.org. The Center's site is an easy-to-use gateway to a wide range of philanthropic information resources. Visitors to the site can readily access many other Web sites, including those maintained by private, corporate, and community foundations; nonprofit organizations; government agencies; and other groups that provide information of interest to nonprofit organizations. For more in-depth information on mining the many Web resources for grantseekers, see *The Foundation Center's Guide to Grantseeking on the Web.* This guide identifies useful sites for grantseekers and provides the "how-tos" of connecting to and effectively using the Internet for funding research.

At the Foundation Center's home page you will find a link to the "Search Zone." The Search Zone provides access to all search mechanisms at the Center's Web site from one central location, along with recommendations for the best search strategy to find the information you seek. Also at this Web site you will find *Philanthropy News Digest* (*PND*), the Center's online news abstracting service of philanthropy-related articles. Besides keeping grantseekers and others abreast of recent and significant developments in the world of philanthropy,

PND also includes Web site and/or book reviews, interviews with prominent newsmakers, spotlights on various nonprofit organizations, an RFP Bulletin, a job corner, a conference calendar, original articles, and more.

The information on the Internet, and the tools used to search it, are constantly changing. Because there is no overall editorial oversight of the information available online, you must evaluate the accuracy and scope of that information yourself. For these and other reasons, it remains a good idea to use the Internet as a supplement to traditional research methods and not to rely on it entirely.

Guidelines

Many of the larger private foundations, and most community foundations, issue guidelines, sometimes in pamphlet form but often as a section of their annual report. More than 2,400 grantmakers now have Web sites, where guidelines are often posted. Many more are likely to have Web sites in the near future. Foundation trustees and staff generally care deeply about the problems of society and struggle to determine the most effective strategies they can use to produce the greatest impact with their funding dollars. When they issue guidelines or announce areas of programmatic interests, these are the result of careful planning and strategy. You should thoroughly review any available guidelines as part of your investigation of a foundation or corporate donor. Some guidelines are very specific, stating goals or even projects to be funded within each area of interest. Others are more general and require further investigation.

If, for example, the foundation in question supports only medical research in Kenya, and your agency provides after-school reading programs for children in Columbus, Ohio, obviously, this is not a good prospect. However, if you are doing medical research at Stanford University that has implications for the population in Africa, there is a chance that the foundation might be interested in your work, if not now, then perhaps in the future.

Don't assume that a funder's guidelines from two years ago are still applicable today, particularly when a funder's assets base has changed or it is experiencing a change in leadership. While the foundation probably will not shift its area of interest overnight from the arts to medicine, there may well be subtle shifts in emphasis. You need to be fully aware of these before making your request.

For information on grants available, you should refer to requests for proposals (RFPs), an increasingly popular vehicle for foundations to publicize new program initiatives. Links to recently posted foundation RFPs are a feature of *Philanthropy News Digest* at the Center's Web site. The Center's *RFP Bulletin* is a weekly listing of current funding opportunities offered by foundations and other grant-making organizations and is delivered to your e-mail box at no charge.

Foundation Web Sites

Today more and more foundations and corporate giving programs have a presence on the Internet. The Foundation Center's Web site currently provides a comprehensive list of annotated links to the Web sites of foundations, corporate grantmakers, and grantmaking public charities. While the vast majority of foundations do not yet have Web sites, those that do maintain Web sites provide much of the information grantseekers have come to expect from print sources, such as annual reports, grants lists, application guidelines, and so forth. Some foundations post their annual reports *only* on the Web. Foundations are making enormous strides in utilizing technology, and grantseekers should be sure to explore existing and emerging Web resources.

The Foundation Center helps grantseekers identify which foundations and corporate giving programs have Web sites by several means. The Center's own Web site, via Grantmaker Web Sites and Foundation Finder, has links to the home pages of foundations or corporate giving programs that have Web sites. Also, *The Foundation Directory Online* and *FC Search: The Foundation Center's Database on CD-ROM* allow you to link directly from a grantmaker record to its Web site.

The Annual Report

A foundation's annual report may prove to be a valuable tool in researching a funder. It is important not only for determining current giving patterns but also for anticipating future trends. The annual report reflects the personality, style, and interests of the foundation.

In reading an annual report, you should look most closely at two sections. First, read the statement by the chairman, president, or chief executive. Look for clues that reveal the foundation's underlying philosophy. What are the problems in society that the foundation wants to address? What kind of impact does its leadership hope to make with the foundation's funds? This section will also reveal if the foundation is in the process of changing direction. Such a shift presents you with a significant window of opportunity, if your project happens to fit within new areas the foundation intends to explore.

The other section to examine is the list of grantees for the past year or years. Check the grants list against what the foundation *says* it wants to fund. You are looking for clues that will illustrate specific areas of interest. You also want to look for any discrepancies. Do they say, for instance, that they don't fund capital campaigns, yet right there in the grants list is a donation of $75,000 to the St. Clairesville Community Center to build a new gymnasium? This doesn't necessarily mean that you should keep them on your prospect list for your own gymnasium. It does mean that you should research the foundation further. Many foundations fund projects or agencies with special connections to the foundation or in which their trustees have a particular interest, even though they fall outside their stated guidelines.

The 990-PF will not give you as much information about a foundation as its Web site or annual report will, but if those are lacking, it is the place you can turn to find a foundation's grants list. For small, locally oriented foundations, the 990-PF may be the *only* source of details on grants awarded, because fewer than 1,600 foundations issue separate annual reports.

Refine

With information in hand about each foundation or corporation on your original list, you are now ready to refine your prospect list. Take care at this stage to focus only on those sources that are *most likely* to help your nonprofit now or in the future. Then ask yourself:

- Have I developed a thorough, well-rounded prospect list?

- Is it targeted? Given the need and the time I have to devote to fundraising, is the list too long or too short?

As you winnow your list, one question will arise: Does my project need to fit precisely within a funder's stated guidelines? Guidelines often indicate a particular area of interest, but they should not be viewed as exclusionary documents. A funder may be considering changing its areas of support precisely at the time your proposal arrives; or someone at the foundation might have some special interest in your project. Each foundation or corporate funder is unique and responds accordingly. Elan Garonzik of the Charles Stewart Mott Foundation notes, "Every foundation is different and has its own personality. It's part of the grantseeker's job to research what that is." Use your common sense when determining whether it is too much of a stretch to go to the next step in exploring a particular funder.

11

Contacting and Cultivating Potential Funders

Making the Initial Contact

Once you have determined that a foundation is a likely funder, then you must initiate contact. Some foundations prefer that you call first to see if your project fits their specific guidelines. Be aware, however, that this is not a popular step with all funders.

If you decide to call first, be sure you don't appear to be going on a fishing expedition. Funders find this particularly annoying. Your conversation needs to make it clear that you have read the guidelines and want further clarification on whether your particular project would fit. You are *not* making a solicitation by telephone.

Funders caution that, if you do call, listen carefully to what is being said. Ilene Mack of the William Randolph Hearst Foundation commented, "I am happy to have a conversation with a grantseeker.

This way I can understand what kind of organization they are and if we are an appropriate fit."

On the other hand, Ms. Mack also cautions the grantseeker to be careful to "listen for the 'no.' "

There are three objectives to the initial call:

- It promotes name recognition of your group.
- It tests the possible compatibility between the potential funder and your agency.
- It permits you to gather additional information about the funder and about possible reaction to your project *before* you actually submit your proposal.

How should you proceed? First, rehearse what you will say about your organization. You may be given just a few minutes by the foundation or corporate representative. Also, have on hand the background information you have compiled about the potential funder and how much and what you would like them to fund. If there is a prior relationship with your nonprofit group, be fully aware of the details. David Gibbs of the Community Foundation for Greater Atlanta notes, "An informed grantseeker gives a different sense to the conversation. This person is seeking guidance and clarification as opposed to being on a fishing expedition. It is easy to respond to this type of inquiry even when you are busy."

Second, make the call. It would be great if you could speak directly with the president of the foundation or senior vice president in charge of corporate contributions. But this will not often happen. Be satisfied with anyone who can respond to your questions. In the process, don't underestimate the importance of support staff. They can be very helpful. They can provide you with key information and ensure that your proposal is processed promptly. Be sure to obtain the name of the person you do speak with so that reference to this conversation can be made when you submit your formal request. This may be your contact person for future calls and letters.

What should you say? Be prepared to:

- Introduce your agency: give the name, location, purpose, and goals.
- State up front why you are calling: You have done your homework. You believe there is a fit between the grantmaker and your organization.

- Inquire if you can submit a proposal: be specific about which one and the hoped-for level of support.

- Request an appointment: few funders are willing to grant the request for a meeting without at least an initial proposal on the table, but it's always worth inquiring about this. As a matter of fact, each time you speak with a funder, you should ask if a face-to-face conversation would be appropriate.

Variations will emerge in each call, so you must be sharp, alert, and ready to respond. At the same time, try to seem relaxed and confident as the discussion proceeds. Remember that you are a potential partner for the prospective funder.

Many foundations have no staff or limited office support. Some corporations assign their philanthropic activities to executives with very heavy workloads. The point is, repeated calls may go unanswered. Above all, be persistent. Persistence will set your agency apart from many nonprofits whose leaders initiate fundraising with determination but quickly lose heart. If you cannot get through to a potential funder on the telephone, send a letter of inquiry designed to gain the same information as the call. If your letter goes unanswered, then be prepared to submit a request anyway.

While some program officers will not meet with applicants until a proposal has been submitted, others say that they would prefer the proposal to be submitted only after a meeting. Hildy Simmons, formerly of J.P. Morgan Private Bank, notes, "We manage expectations by communicating responsiveness to those who are asking. This starts with a brief telephone conversation and concludes with a face-to-face meeting, if the application is competitive."

The message here is that, like people, every foundation is different. Foundations, in fact, are made up of people. It is important to listen to and to respect what the funding representative is telling you about preferred styles of approach.

The Letter of Intent

Many grantmakers today are requesting that applicants provide a brief letter of inquiry or intent about their project *before* submitting a complete proposal. Just like the introductory phone call, this letter is used by funders as a simple screening device, enabling the grantmaker to preclude submission of an inappropriate application and to encourage the submission of proposals with funding potential. It also enables those grants decision makers who prefer to be involved in the shaping of a proposal at the very earliest stages to do so. The letter of intent can be useful to the grantseeker, since it saves time compiling lengthy documents and attachments for proposals that are unlikely to be favorably received.

The requirement to submit a preliminary letter of intent is not always a plus for the grantseeker. In the first place, it is an extra step, requiring that additional time be factored into the application cycle. Second, some view this procedure as a way for the funder to cut off an application before the grantseeker has had the opportunity to fully portray the benefits of the project. And finally, you need to have the full proposal, at least in draft form, before you can submit a letter of intent, which in a sense is a highly compacted proposal with most of the components covered, albeit briefly. As David Gibbs of the Community Foundation for Greater Atlanta tells us, "The letter of inquiry can be valuable and useful for both sides. It is easier for the nonprofit organization to pull together than a full proposal. The grantmaker can assess quickly if the project meets guidelines, criteria, and interests."

A talent for précis writing is definitely required to get the letter of intent just right. It should not be longer than two to three pages.

What follows is a letter of intent from the American Institute of Chemical Engineers to the Russell Family Foundation:

August 12, 2003

Stephanie Anderson
Grants Manager
The Russell Family Foundation
P.O. Box 2567
Gig Harbor, WA 98335

Dear Ms. Anderson:

On behalf of the American Institute of Chemical Engineers (AIChE), please accept this letter of inquiry outlining our newest initiative, the *AIChE Institute for Sustainability*. It is our hope that the Russell Family Foundation will consider a full proposal requesting a grant of $100,000 to support the start-up and development of this new Institute, which will address social, industrial, and global needs for awareness and training in sustainable development.

Founded in 1908, AIChE is a professional association of more than 50,000 members that provides leadership in advancing the chemical engineering profession. An essential role of chemical engineers is to use their scientific and technical knowledge to develop processes and to design and operate plants to make useful products at a reasonable cost and in a safe, efficient, and environmentally sound manner. Today, a shift toward sustainable practices supports chemical engineering efforts in waste reduction, emissions control, and remediation.

Chemical engineers play a major role in the innovation and development of varied products and services. Chemical engineers work in nearly every industrial sector, creating, re-creating, enhancing, refining, and re-defining chemicals, materials, fuels, drugs, food, and water. The historical challenge has been how to produce while being efficient and economical in stewardship of natural and other resources. As consumer demands escalate, the challenges multiply. How can chemical engineers improve the health and well being of mankind, nurture economic growth, and reconcile the natural resource, business, and societal implications of achieving this goal?

The *AIChE Institute for Sustainability* will promote awareness of the scientific and engineering challenges of sustainability, develop practices and tools that will guide the creation of more sustainable manufacturing processes, and support and encourage chemical engineers' contributions toward meeting the growing environmental concerns of our society.

The *Institute for Sustainability* will concentrate its expertise on industrial ecology, sustainable business practices, and international sustainable development. It is designed to be an action-oriented institution, as opposed to a "think tank" or advisory group. Additionally, the Institute will certify engineers and scientists in sustainability and safe environment practices, provide industry with financial metrics for measuring industry sustainability (while improving current cost assessment and sustainability metrics). Finally, the Institute will also develop innovative K–12 and undergraduate science and engineering curricula by incorporating "green" engineering and sustainability concepts.

AIChE's Institute for Sustainability is comprised of three distinct centers. Each center addresses a unique audience with pertinent programming, education, training, stewardship, and government relations. The centers are:

- The *Center for Sustainable Technology and Practice* will focus on industry; promoting the efficient use of energy and materials in product/industrial systems planning and design.

- The *Center for Environmental Excellence* will target the individual practicing engineer or scientist; educate and train the professional on concepts of reduced energy and material usage, implications of design on the environment, and other methods to achieve environmental excellence.

- The *Center for Social Stewardship* will concentrate its products and services on ameliorating societal concerns regarding international sustainable development, community and school outreach, and public perceptions of chemical engineering and environmental issues.

AIChE will capitalize on the expertise of existing staff as a foundation for developing the tools to address sustainability issues. In addition, a Director, a Project Manager, and an Associate will be allocated to run its daily operations and manage the long-term goals.

The *Institute for Sustainability* will be a catalyst for driving the development and deployment of new technologies and practices that are needed to shape a world that can truly sustain future generations. Through multidisciplinary partnerships with engineering and scientific societies worldwide, government entities and NGOs, the Institute will work to deliver technically viable, commercially feasible and environmentally and socially sustainable solutions to meet the challenges of tomorrow.

I would be happy to submit a full proposal further describing the Institute and its initiatives at your request. If you have any questions regarding the project, AIChE, or our request, I invite you to call me at 212-591-7660.

Thank you for your thoughtful consideration of this request. I look forward to speaking with you.
Sincerely,

Scott Hamilton
Director of Planning, Development & Corporate Communications

Some grantmakers have online application forms that function as letters of inquiry. What follows is a screen from the online grant application used by the W. K. Kellogg Foundation:

While the letter of intent has its pros and cons from the grantseeker's perspective, this is still required by many funders as a preliminary step in the process. And writing such a letter is a skill that proposal writers need to develop.

Submitting the Proposal

Actually submitting the proposal may seem anticlimactic considering the amount of preparation that has gone into identifying and researching the prospective funders and putting together the various components. But once you have determined that a meeting prior to submission is not possible or is unnecessary, or once you've had the desired meeting, eventually there comes the time to submit the full proposal to the funders on your list.

Checklists may prove useful at this point. You may wish to check and double-check one last time to ensure that all requirements of the funder have been met and that all of the pieces of the proposal package are there in the proper sequence. Above all, you will want to be sure that you submit the proposal in accordance with the funder's deadline. If possible, whether you use regular mail, e-mail, or are applying online, send in your proposal at least two weeks in advance of the deadline. This enables the funder to request additional information, if needed.

Grantseekers often wonder whether they should mail in their proposals, send by overnight mail or messenger, or hand-deliver them. By far the best choice is the least expensive one. Use regular mail unless there is a very good reason to do otherwise.

Cultivating the Potential Funder

Don't forget to continue to communicate once you have submitted your proposal. Cultivation of the funding prospect can make the critical difference between getting a grant and getting lost in the shuffle.

Knowledge of the funder's situation, and of that particular grantmaker's procedures for processing proposals, can be extremely helpful in developing your cultivation strategy.

Funders are flooded with proposals. Even if they turn down all that are clearly outside their guidelines, they still get many more than their budgets will allow them to fund. To cite just one example, John Marshall of the Kresge Foundation points out, "We receive 600 applications per year. 450 are declined; 150 are funded."

How can you assure that your proposal will be one of those to get into the grant pipeline? The ways in which foundations operate differ widely. At some small family foundations, the donor himself or herself will review all requests. At the larger foundations, a first cut is usually made to eliminate those that are out of program, then program officers review proposals in specific areas and must take each proposal through a staff review process before a recommendation goes to their board of trustees. Andrew Lark describes the Frances L. & Edwin L. Cummings Memorial Fund's process as follows: "There is an immediate rejection if a request is out of our funding guidelines. We generally ask those being considered to fill out a Cummings Fund questionnaire form. Then we do site visits. We look for efficiency in the way they run the program, realism in the application, and strong board/management involvement."

Foundations frequently work closely with the grantseeker in developing the request. Jim DeNova of the Claude Worthington Benedum Foundation states, "We prefer to get involved as early as possible." And David Egner of the Hudson-Webber Foundation says, "Build the relationship. Connect with and cultivate the grantmaker." Elan Garonzik of the Charles Stewart Mott Foundation helps us understand the importance of that relationship: "A large percent of applications we support do not come in cold over the transom. We have a pre-existing relationship with the organization. We know their people. They understand what we are looking for in a grantee."

John Marshall of the Kresge Foundation summarizes the challenge facing nonprofit grantseekers: "Agencies have to make informed choices about the sources to which they will apply. Then they need to follow that up with good communication and a carefully constructed application. Speed doesn't take the place of judgment."

Several forms of cultivation may be particularly valuable after the proposal is submitted:

- Communication by phone or e-mail;
- Face-to-face meetings;
- Using board contacts; and
- Written updates and progress reports.

Communication by Phone or E-mail

Normally you should plan to call or send an e-mail about two weeks after the proposal package is mailed. The primary purpose of this communication is to make sure that the proposal has been received. You have requested a meeting in the cover letter and offered to supply any additional information required to help the funder consider your request. You should therefore ask if it is appropriate to schedule a meeting at the foundation or corporate office or a site visit at your agency. Be sure to ask about the process and timing for the review of your proposal. This will guide you as to when you might call back or send updated information.

Call periodically thereafter to check on the status of your proposal. If you have had no response in the expected time frame, call to find out if there has been a change in the schedule. Ask the same types of questions as you did previously: Is additional information required? When will the proposal be reviewed? Would the foundation or corporate representative like to meet? Be brief. There is a fine line between being helpful and being too pushy.

Each time you call, be prepared to answer the program officer's detailed questions about any aspect of the proposal or of your agency's work. You should also expect to receive calls or e-mails from your program officer during the course of the proposal review.

Hunter Corbin of the Hyde and Watson Foundation warns the grantseeker that it frustrates the funder "when you call the nonprofit, and no one knows what the application is all about. Worse, you call the organization and request information, and no one calls you back."

It helps to stay in touch by phone or e-mail. This gives you a chance to find out what is happening with your proposal and to share information with the foundation or corporate funder.

When appropriate, follow up the phone conversation with a note or e-mail message about the next step you plan to take or confirming any new information you provided over the phone. While phone communication is often the most convenient way to keep in touch, you need to be sure that any agreement or information that is critical to a successful outcome of the review process is put in writing.

Face-to-Face Meetings

Appointments can be very hard to obtain and typically occur at the initiative of the grantmaker. Many funders will not agree to a meeting until the proposal is under active consideration. This might entail assigning it to a program officer, who would then be the person to meet with you. Even when the foundation or corporate representative is intensely interested in your project, he or she may believe that a meeting would not be helpful in arriving at a recommendation on your request. However, some foundations insist on a site visit for most or all of the groups to which they make grants.

When you are offered an appointment, you should view this as a very special opportunity. It is one that you must prepare for carefully. David Odahowski of the Edyth Bush Charitable Foundation underscores the importance of the meeting: "Every request that goes to the Board entails a visit."

First, be sure that the right team is selected to attend the meeting. If your nonprofit agency has staff, the chief executive officer or executive director should go. The CEO should be able to answer specific questions relating to the project. The other member of the team should be a volunteer, preferably from the board. The presence of the volunteer underscores the fact that the board is aware of and supports the work of the organization. Under the right circumstances, a member of the program staff can be a helpful adjunct, or you might bring along someone who benefits from the good work of your organization. But don't overwhelm the funder by bringing too many additional people to the meeting. Clear with the funding representative precisely how many people are welcome. If time permits, call a day in advance to confirm the date and remind the funder who is coming. Invite the prospective funder to visit your organization. A site visit obviously allows you to introduce the funding representative to a wider range of people involved in your agency or project.

Next, prepare for the meeting. Compile background information about the foundation or corporation. You should be careful to note any prior interaction with the funder, especially if it was less than positive. Develop a profile of the person(s) with whom you are meeting, if this information is available in standard biographical sources, on the Web, or via the grapevine. Your peers in the nonprofit world who are grant recipients might shed some light on the personality and idiosyncracies of the funder.

Create a role for each of the participants. It is critical that no one sits idle. There should be a dialogue and rapport among the meeting participants.

Last, know precisely what you want to accomplish in the meeting. You won't leave with a check in hand, but you do need to decide in advance what information you want to share and to obtain. David Grant of the Geraldine Rockefeller Dodge Foundation addresses preparedness: "There is an art to the interview. Be prepared. Be on time."

You should expect to accomplish a great deal through the simple process of meeting face-to-face with the funder. The meeting will establish a personal relationship between the representatives of your organization and of the funding agency. Despite our high-tech world, giving is still a highly personal activity. Hence, the better your rapport with the donor, the more likely it is that financial support will be forthcoming.

Along with getting to know the people at your agency, this will be an opportunity for the funding representative to gain a much better understanding of your group's work. Hearing from knowledgeable people about your mission, programs, and dreams will allow the funder to ask questions, to refine information, and to correct misperceptions.

E. Belvin Williams of the Turrell Fund describes what the grant-maker seeks to achieve at a face-to-face meeting. "We go armed with an agenda. That is, having reviewed the proposal, we have questions and ideas in mind. We look for the ability to deal with challenges, perseverance, creativity, and problem-solving skills among the representatives of the nonprofit. In the course of the meeting, we notice things that can't necessarily be written about."

The staff and trustees of the Frances L. & Edwin L. Cummings Memorial Fund shared the following evaluation form, detailing the questions they ask themselves concerning a face-to-face meeting:

THE FRANCES L. & EDWIN L. CUMMINGS MEMORIAL FUND TRUSTEE'S SITE VISIT EVALUATION

I. GENERAL INFORMATION

1. Name of Organization:

   Location:

   Date of site visit:

   Other Attendees:

II. PROGRAM INFORMATION:

1. Rate Executive Director with respect to the following:
    (Scale: 1=Excellent, 2=Very Good, 3=Good, 4=Fair, 5=Poor)

    ___ Understanding of his/her job

    ___ Leadership

    ___ Relationship to staff

    ___ Understanding of needs of community being served

    ___ Effective communicator of ideas

    ___ Dedication to job

    ___ Ability to respond under pressure—deal with critical
    problems

    Additional comments: _____

    _____

    _____

2. Is the organization overloaded with professionals, properly
    lean, or understaffed for program efficiency? _____

    _____

    _____

    _____

3. Does this organization have a proven track record in gen-
    eral? Specifically as to this program(s)? _____

    _____

    _____

    _____

4. Does this organization have the potential to expand to meet
    increasing needs of the community? (If this organization is
    already expanding/expanded, has it done so in a manage-
    able fashion?) _____

    _____

    _____

    _____

5. Is this organization offering innovative programs or are they replicating/duplicating others' efforts?_____

_____

_____

_____

III. BOARD OF DIRECTORS:

1. Is the Board of Directors an "active" or a "paper" Board? Explain. _____

_____

_____

_____

2. Using the same scale as above, rank the Board of Directors with respect to:

___ Leadership

___ Relationship to staff

___ Dedication to achieving stated objectives of the organization

___ Personal knowledge of organization's daily activities

___ Amount of time personally committed to organization

___ Personal financial commitment

___ Distribution of responsibility among Board Members

Additional Comments: _____

_____

_____

_____

IV. FACILITIES:

1. Is the space effectively utilized?   Yes ___   No ___
Describe. _____

_____

_____

2. Is the atmosphere conducive to the programs being oper-
   ated? Yes _____ No _____

   If no, please explain. _____

   _____

   _____

   _____

V. PROPOSAL INFORMATION:

1. Is there a need for this kind of service in the community?
   Are other agencies already providing the same kind of ser-
   vice(s)? If so, is the proposal(s) unique in any respect? _____

   _____

   _____

   _____

2. Are the goals of the proposal(s) aggressive enough? Too
   aggressive? _____

   _____

   _____

   _____

3. Is the budget for the proposal(s) realistic? _____

   _____

   _____

   _____

4. Is the proposal(s) cost-effective in its anticipated results?

   _____

   _____

   _____

5. Has the program(s) been well planned? _____

   _____

   _____

   _____

6. Is the Board/Staff committed to undertaking the project(s) regardless of Cummings Fund support? (If so, how?)

_____

_____

_____

VI. FINANCIAL INFORMATION:

1. What is the overall present financial situation in this organization? _____

_____

_____

_____

_____

2. Additional Comments/Summary: _____

_____

_____

_____

_____

_____

_____

During a face-to-face meeting, the funder will gain a much better sense of the project for which you are seeking support. Critical information about the proposal, such as the need, methods for addressing it, and the capability of your group to run the program, might be covered during discussion. For this reason, be sure to review the proposal carefully before the meeting.

You must assume responsibility for the agenda of the meeting. Be prepared to:

- Use an icebreaker. The first few times you attend a meeting with a funder, it can be nerve-racking. Break the tension by telling an amusing anecdote, by relaying a true incident of interest to the group, or by commenting about the view or an object in the room where the meeting takes place.

- Introduce all of the meeting participants by name, title, and/or role. This way the funder will know the players and be clear to whom specific questions should be addressed.

- Get down to business. Once introduced, the participants should promptly move on to the real purpose of the meeting: Your group hopes the funder will become a partner with you in getting your project off the ground.

- Remind the funder about the mission and history of your agency. Be thorough but brief in this review.

- Describe the programs you offer. Again, be succinct, but be certain that the funder has a good overview of your services. This is important in case the project submitted for funding proves not to be of interest. The funder may request a proposal relating to a different aspect of your agency's work, having achieved a good grasp of the whole program.

- Describe the project for which you are seeking support. It is critical that you demonstrate the conviction that success is likely. Provide the necessary detail for the funder to understand the problem being addressed and your agency's proposed response to it.

- Keep a dialogue going. It is easy to speak at length about your organization. But it is also easy to bore the funders and, even worse, for you to come away from the meeting not having gained any relevant new information about this grantmaker. Whenever possible, try to elicit the funder's reactions. Inquire about current programs they have funded that address similar problems. Treat the grantmaker as a potential partner. Remember, their dollars have significance only when combined with programs. Listen carefully to their responses, comments, and questions. This dialogue will clue you into the *real* interests and concerns of this potential funder. Don't assume anything.

- Obtain a clear understanding of the next steps. You should determine the following: if anything more is needed for review of the request; when the proposal will come up for review; and how the agency will be notified about the outcome. If, as a result of this conversation, it is clear that the proposal is unlikely to be funded, you should ask what you might do to resubmit this or another proposal.

A great deal can be accomplished in a well-crafted meeting, whether at their place or yours. You don't want this process spoiled by extending it for too long. Once it is clear that the objectives have been achieved, you need to summarize the next steps to be taken by both sides and move on to a cordial goodbye. End the meeting while the "good vibes" are still being felt by both sides.

Using Board Contacts

A contact from one of your board members with a peer affiliated with the foundation or corporate funder you are approaching will usually reinforce the relationship you are building.

How do you discover if your board members have contacts that can help with raising funds? First, circulate to all of the members of your board the names of the officers and directors of the foundations and corporations you plan to approach. Ask your board members to respond to you by a certain date about those whom they know. Then work one-on-one with individual board members, building a strategy for them to utilize their contacts. Another approach is to meet with the board members to talk about individuals with whom they can be helpful. You may find contacts with funders that you had not intended to approach, where having an entree will make a difference.

Knowing that you have board-to-board contact is not enough. You must assist your board member in capitalizing on this relationship on behalf of your nonprofit group. First, develop a scenario with the board member focusing on how to approach the contact. The more personal the approach, the better it is. Second, assist your board member with understanding why this funder would want to help your organization, finding the right language to discuss your agency and your funding needs, and drafting correspondence as needed. Then make sure that the board member makes the promised contact after the proposal has been submitted. Periodically remind this individual of the next step to be taken. The groundwork you have done is wasted if the board member never follows through.

Be forewarned that staff of foundations and corporate grant-makers may be concerned about your board members contacting their board members. This is particularly true of professionally staffed foundations where program officers may consider it inappropriate or may view it as interference. Some funders feel strongly that an agency should not use a board contact, even if they have one.

Still others report that their trustees are encouraged to indicate their interest in a project. At a minimum, staff want to know in advance that a board contact will be used. Larry Kressley of the Public Welfare Foundation advises, "This kind of contact does happen. Sometimes nonprofits play their hand too strongly. A heads-up to the staff is helpful. Watch out for politics and egos."

Where you already are in contact with the foundation staff, it is critical to discuss a board contact with them before it is set in motion. Finally, keep in mind that relying on board contacts can backfire. At some foundations, if a board member has had contact with an agency, he or she is expected to disqualify himself from discussion about the specific proposal.

Written Updates and Progress Reports

Written communication helps a foundation or corporate donor learn more about your group and reminds them that you need their support. You should plan to send materials selectively while your proposal is under review. Here are some ideas for what you might send:

- summary reports on what is going on in your organization;
- financial information, such as a new audit;
- newsletters, bulletins, brochures, or other frequently issued information;
- updates/reports on specific projects; and
- newspaper or magazine articles on the project for which you have requested support, the work of your nonprofit, or closely related issues.

It is usually not necessary to customize the materials, but a brief accompanying note always helps to reinforce your relationship with the funder.

Here is an example of an update letter.

July 24, 2003

Mr. J. Andrew Lark
The Frances L. & Edwin L. Cummings Memorial Fund
501 Fifth Avenue
Suite #708
New York, NY 10017

Dear Mr. Lark:

I wanted to share the enclosed photos of our recent graduation cere-mony at South Brooklyn Community High School because you have played such an important role in our achievements.

As you may know, this has been a milestone year in the history of South Brooklyn Community High School, which became an inde-pendent high school last September, and so our graduation event took on special significance. It represented the culmination of our yearlong transformation into a model, independent high school and, for the first time, we were able to award official South Brooklyn Community High School diplomas. The evening also underscored how much we have accomplished since we launched the capital campaign to build our new Good Shepherd Services Center, where South Brooklyn Com-munity High School is housed.

Twenty-two young people, who had formerly been truant or dropped out of school, passed rigorous NYS Regents exams and earned their high school diplomas. We were honored to have several speakers attend the graduation ceremony including NYS Senator Velmanette Montgomery, Charles Amundson, Deputy Superinten-dent of BASIS and Michelle Cahill, Senior Counselor to the Chancellor for Education Policy at the Department of Education.

I hope that the pictures help capture the significance of this historic occasion and the impact that South Brooklyn Community High School has on our young people. We are so grateful for your generous support that has made these achievements possible.

Sincerely,

Sr. Paulette LoMonaco
Executive Director

E-mail Communication

Don't overlook the possibility of selective e-mail contact with prospective funders, if they have communicated with you that way in the past or have indicated a preference for this vehicle for providing updates. A concise e-mail message with, perhaps, a link to an appropriate area of your Web site or other Internet coverage of your activities, can have a significant impact. Repeated or unnecessary e-mail messages directed at funding program officers can prove annoying, however.

Some agencies have developed listservs or broadcast e-mail services to keep various constituents apprised of recent developments. It would be wise *not* to add a funder's e-mail address to your listserv without prior permission to do so. On the other hand, this is a very convenient way to keep donors and prospective funders aware of your agency's accomplishments if they agree to it.

In general cultivation is welcomed by today's grantmaker. As Elizabeth Smith of the Hyams Foundation urges, "Talk to us! We appreciate receiving newsletters and periodic updates, including when a grantee or applicant may be facing changes." And E. Belvin Williams of the Turrell Fund adds, ". . . especially if it really helps us in making a decision."

Even after your project has concluded, don't forget to continue to cultivate your donors. Fundraising is all about relationship building. In the words of Joel Orosz of the W. K. Kellogg Foundation, "We expect to stay in touch with former grantees. Sometimes as a result of communication with them, an idea surfaces in which we have an interest. If this happens, we will encourage the submission of a proposal."

12

Life after the Grant — or Rejection

The Initial Follow-up to a Grant

You've just received a grant from a foundation or corporation. Congratulations! What should you do? First of all, you should celebrate. Include everyone in your agency who contributed to this wonderful outcome. Thank them for their help and remind them about what this means for your organization.

Next, send a thank you letter to your funder. This seems so obvious that one would think it hardly worth stating. Yet a number of the grantmakers interviewed for this book responded to the question, "What is the best thing an organization can do after receiving a grant?" with the simple response: send a thank you letter.

Here are two samples. The first is the very short thank you letter that the Foundation Center sends to all of its basic support donors. This satisfies most foundations' requirements and ultimately winds up in each donor's grantee file for the Center. It is highly customizable so that one can substitute, for example, "renewed" or "increased" for "continued" in the second sentence and "pledge" for "contribution" if the foundation's grant letter does not come with a check. It is also possible, of course, to add additional text specific to the request, the project, or the audience that will benefit, as appropriate.

Date

Contact
Title
Organzation
Address

Grant #

Greeting:

Thank you for the _____'s contribution of $$$ to the Foundation Center for 2004. We appreciate your continued support at a time when grantmakers are faced with increased demand on their resources and nonprofits are relying on our free programs and services more than ever.

We will report back to you on your gift through our 2004 Annual Report, which will be available in mid-2005. Please let us know if we can be of any assistance in the meantime.

Sincerely,

April 15, 2003

Ms. Ruth Shack, President
Dade Community Foundation
200 South Biscayne Boulevard, Suite 2780
Miami, FL 33131-2343

Dear Ms. Shack:

Please forgive my tardiness in formally thanking the Foundation for its recent decision to again fund Sembrando Flores in the Discretionary Grant category. What a couple of years we have seen; it's been a whirlwind of activity, with so many positive developments. . . and more to come!

I remember saying about this time last year that your Discretionary Grant funds came at such a crucial time; again, this year, this proves true. Though Sembrando is stronger and a bit larger this time around, we are also trying to do so much more. The Foundation's funds are indeed, still crucial. Your confidence in granting us ATREVETE under the Partnership Grant last year, and in assisting us with basic expenses under this—Project Seed—was most timely and needed.

I also want to thank the Foundation for its sponsorship of our trip to the recent San Francisco Conference; it gave us all an excellent opportunity for input and perspective on a national level. We look forward to continuing to explore the possibilities of providing fresh approaches to HIV/AIDS Prevention programs, especially as they impact Latinos in South Dade. We are now about half-way through our Ryan White Title III Planning and Assessment Grant, and we are cautiously optimistic that a second year will be awarded; this will help us in the short run understand the nature of the problem better, and in the long one how we can work towards improving services.

Again, let me express how much we appreciate both your support and the opportunity to further develop our possibilities.

Yours, in Good Faith,

Nancy Rivera, Director

The foundation representatives we interviewed expressed a concern that needs to be taken to heart. Appreciate the investment that has just been made in your agency. Recognize that it is not just an institution that is supporting you but the actual people within that institution. Remember that the grants decision makers feel good about the commitment to invest in your organization. They may even have had to fight for you in the face of opposition by other staff and board members. Show your thanks and appreciation for this vote of confidence.

Grantmakers want to ensure effective communication after a grant is awarded. They remind us that a grant is a contract to undertake a specific set of activities, and they want and need to know what has transpired.

Remember the watchword of all fundraising: communication. A telephone call to say "thank you," an update on recent activities, or an announcement of additional funding committed or received are all ways to keep in touch after the grant is made.

Grant Reporting

If a foundation has specific reporting requirements, you will be told what they are. Usually reporting requirements are included in the grant letter; sometimes you are asked to sign and return a copy of the grant letter or of a separate grant contract. These "conditions," which a representative of the nonprofit signs, sometimes require timely reports that are tied to payments.

Here is the Conditions of Grant and Request for Payment form which describes the Flinn Foundation's legal and reporting conditions:

Flinn Foundation
Conditions of Grant and Request for Payment Form

For the Foundation to proceed with payment of the grant funds authorized, the Conditions of Grant statement must be reviewed and the Request for Payment Form signed by the recipient organization's chief officer, and returned to the Foundation. Signature of this form by the chief officer of a grantee organization (CEO, dean of school or head of an academic unit) constitutes review and acceptance of the conditions specified.

Initial payment of grant funds (generally, two payments on grants of up to $25,000 or less; no more than the first three months of project activity costs of multi-year grants) will be made upon presentation of this signed and completed form to the Foundation, plus submission by the project director (the individual directly responsible for developing and guiding the funded activity) of a project implementation schedule and budget detailing how these initial grant funds will be spent.

Evidence of readiness to initiate project activity in keeping with the intent of the grant award must be submitted for the Foundation to release grant funds. If a significant portion of grant funds are to be used to pay the salary of professional staff not yet hired or to pay the contract of a consultant or vendor, the project director must submit documentation of the employee hire (CV and start date) and/or copies of the signed and dated contracts with consultants or vendors before initial payment will be made.

These documents will be reviewed by Foundation staff and, if found to be consistent with the intent of the grant, payment will be made within thirty (30) days of receipt. All grant payment checks will be mailed by the Foundation to the address shown on this form. No grant checks will be delivered personally nor, for security purposes, will a grant payment check be released to any representative of the grantee organization.

Subsequent payments on multi-year grants and those in excess of $25,000 will be made upon submission by the project director of a line-item expenditure report detailing how initial grant funds were spent. This report should also specify the amount of grant funds needed to support project activity for the subsequent time period. A brief narrative report prepared by the project director, which describes project activity for that time period, must also be submitted with this expenditure report.

Foundation Grant ID number _____

Institutional Grant ID number _____

Duration of Grant Period (total project length):

From _____through _____
     (month, day, year)   (month, day, year)

Total Amount of Approved Grant: $_____

Amount of first payment: $_____ Date Requested:_____

Check to be made payable to: _____

Check to be mailed to (name, title, address): _____

Project Director (name, title, address, telephone, e-mail address): _____

Institutional Project Fiscal Officer (name, title, address, telephone, e-mail address): _____

The conditions of the grant are hereby accepted and agreed to as of the date specified.

By: _____
    (organization's principal officer)

Title: _____

Date: _____

Here is an example of the manner in which the Hyde and Watson Foundation communicates with grantees.

Ladies and Gentlemen:

It is a pleasure to inform you that in response to an appeal dated September 6, 2000, a grant was authorized on October 18, 2000, as specified below:

Grantee: _____
Grant Purpose: Purchase of books and instructional tools
Grant Amount: $10,000.00

This grant was voted payable in the year ending 2000. Enclosed is a check for $10,000.00 which represents payment in full. **By the act of accepting, endorsing, and depositing the check, you confirm the following four statements:**

1. That this Foundation does not control the above-mentioned grantee organization, its projects, or programs;

2. That the grantee organization listed above continues to be tax exempt under Section 501(c)(3) and is "not a private foundation" under Section 509(a) of the Internal Revenue Code (or other appropriate ruling);

3. That the grant funds will not be used in any way which would subject this grantor Foundation to penalty taxes;

4. That a grant/progress report will be forwarded to us as soon as the funds are expended or no later than one year from the date of the enclosed check.

Please note that the grant report (Item 4) is very important. In accordance with our current guidelines, future proposals will be considered at the Grants Committee/Board level only after the required report including confirmation of expenditures of the funds has been received. The report should include the following information:

- A statement confirming that the grant funds have been expended in accordance with the terms of the grant;
- A brief to moderate narrative on the grant project including a statement as to what impact the grant had on the organization and the project itself, along with a financial breakdown of how the grant funds were spent.

On behalf of the Board of Directors of this Foundation, I wish you much success with your endeavors.

Sincerely yours,

Hunter W. Corbin
President

When a foundation provides formal reporting guidelines, in most cases there will be dates when the reports are due. If they have given you specific dates for reporting, develop a tickler system to keep track of them. If you can tell now that you'll have a problem meeting these deadlines (such as your auditors are scheduled for March, and the audited financial report is due in February), discuss this with the funder immediately. If the foundation staff has not heard from the grantee within a reasonable time period after the reports are due, they will call or send the grant recipient a note to follow up.

Some funders want reports at quarterly or six-month intervals, but most request an annual report and/or a final report, two to three months after the conclusion of the project. Even for grants of fairly short duration, foundations often express the desire to receive an interim report. Unless otherwise stated, an interim report can be informal.

The Cleveland Foundation issues very specific reporting instructions. Its *Grant Report Preparation Guidelines* provide a useful framework to guide agency staff in drafting a report to *any* funder. While these guidelines are designed for the Cleveland Foundation's grantees, they provide a reliable model for reports to other foundations that may not be as specific in their requirements.

The following guidelines are reprinted in their totality with permission from the Cleveland Foundation:

THE CLEVELAND FOUNDATION
GRANT REPORT PREPARATION GUIDELINES

OVERVIEW
The Cleveland Foundation, in accordance with its Grant Agreement, requires all grant recipients to prepare periodic narrative and financial reports on project activity and expenditures corresponding to the project's approved budget.

Periodic reports are not only necessary for proper oversight to ensure accountability, but also serve as a valuable learning tool for both Foundation staff and grantees. We greatly appreciate your candor and thoughtful review of your project experience. *Be assured that we do not share these documents with any other organization or funder.*

NARRATIVE AND FINANCIAL REPORTS

- Please refer to your grant award letter for the scheduled due dates of your reports.
- Use the attached forms for both interim and final reports.
- Type your reports and answer all questions in the order listed. **Please complete and attach the Grant Report Cover Sheet to your report.** We suggest that your response not exceed five pages.
- The financial report should include expenditures incurred as well as the balance of Foundation funds not expended through the reporting period. Use parentheses to indicate any budget deficits in the "Balance" column of the form. Each financial report should be signed by the grantee's chief financial officer or chief executive officer.
- Final reports should include a review of performance and activities covering the entire grant period.
- Please send the **original + one copy** of the signed and dated narrative and financial reports in the same envelope, to the attention of the Foundation staff assigned to your grant, per your grant award letter.

RELEASE OF GRANT FUNDS
The Foundation may hold scheduled grant payments until it has received properly completed narrative and financial grant reports. Please refer to **Section 3** of the **Terms and Conditions of Grant** for more information concerning the release of grant funds.

UNEXPENDED FUNDS
Funds that are not expended or encumbered during the grant period should be returned to The Cleveland Foundation unless the Foundation makes written authorization to extend the award beyond the original end date of the grant.

THE CLEVELAND FOUNDATION
GRANT REPORT COVER SHEET

Please check one: ❑ Interim Report ❑ Final Report

Organization Name: _____

Grant Number: _____

Grant Amount:_____

Start Date of Grant Period: _____

End Date of Grant Period: _____

Dates Covered By This Report: From _____ To _____

Project Title: _____

Purpose of Grant: _____

_____

Org. Mailing Address: _____

City, State, Zip:_____

County: _____

Telephone, Fax: _____

Web Address:_____

Executive Director: _____

Board Chair: _____

Project Director: _____

Grant Report Prepared By:

Name *(please print)*: _____

Signature: _____

Date:_____

Telephone:_____

Email:_____

THE CLEVELAND FOUNDATION
GRANT REPORT NARRATIVE REPORT

OVERVIEW

Please answer all the questions in the order listed *(retype the headings and questions provided onto your report)*. Those questions not applicable to your project should be marked N/A.

I. PROJECT INFORMATION

(If more appropriate, you may defer responding to questions five and six until the final report.)

1. Please summarize your original expected outcomes for this project and how you had planned to achieve them.

2. What have been the principal accomplishments of the project to date? How have they been achieved? How have the grant funds been used?

3. The Foundation recognizes that circumstances can change, possibly affecting project implementation. What, if any, difficulties have you encountered; why did they occur; and what refinements or plans have been made to overcome them? Please indicate activities that are behind schedule or not yet begun, and any changes in project plans or personnel.

4. What have been the most challenging or surprising aspects of this project? Have there been any unexpected outcomes?

5. Based on your experience to date, what advice would you give to other organizations planning a similar program? What have been the strengths and limitations of the project? What would you do differently if you had the chance?

6. Please describe your post-grant plans for this project. How will it be financed?

II. ORGANIZATIONAL INFORMATION
It is very helpful to understand the organizational context in which your project is proceeding. Please take this opportunity to update us on any significant organizational changes, developments or challenges. How have these developments contributed to or impeded the success of the project? Additionally, is there any problem or issue confronting your organization requiring technical assistance? If so, would a meeting with Foundation staff be helpful at this time?

III. ATTACHMENTS (optional)
Please attach copies of any public recognition, awards, press releases or news articles pertinent to this project.

THE CLEVELAND FOUNDATION
GRANT REPORT PROJECT FINANCIAL REPORT

Please check one: ❑ Interim Report   ❑ Final Report

Organization Name: _____

Grant Number: _____

Start Date of Grant Period: _____

End Date of Grant Period: _____

Project Title: _____

Dates Covered By This Report: From _____ To _____

	Amount Approved	Amount Expended	Balance
Personnel Expenses			
Salaries and Wages			
Fringe Benefits			
Non-Personnel Expenses			
Contract Services/ Professional Fees			
Office Space			
Equipment/Supplies			
Staff/Board Development			
Travel/Related Expenses			
Indirect Costs			
Other			
Total Project Expenses			

Financial Report Prepared By:

Name *(please print)*: _____

Signature: _____

Date:_____

Telephone:_____

Email:_____

The Cleveland Foundation guidelines are particularly applicable if you have received special project support. Don't be concerned if your project does not lend itself to many of these questions. For instance, if you have received $15,000 to hire a tutor for your after-school program, some of the sections are probably not applicable. Others, like post-grant plans, should be addressed in some fashion in almost any report.

Even if you have received unrestricted, general-purpose support, funders want to know what overall goals you set for your agency for the year. Did you achieve them? What were some specific triumphs? What were some particular problems you faced, and how did you overcome them? Or, are you still dealing with the challenges? (Remember, realism is what counts, along with a sense of confidence that you are appropriately managing the grant.) What follows is a report using the format required by the Hyde and Watson Foundation from World Impact, Inc.

Grant Report Information Sheet

To: Mr. Hunter W. Corbin, President
Grant ID #: 9201564
Grantee/Legal Organization Name: World Impact, Inc.
Address of Organization: 275 Sussex Avenue, Newark, NJ 07107
Telephone Number: 973-483-3833
Fax Number: 973-483-5525
E-mail Address: fclark@worldimpact.org
Name of Executive Officer or Contact Person: Dr. D. Fred Clark
Grant Amount Voted: $20,000
Approval Date: 10/31/2001
Grant Amount Paid: $20,000
Payment Date: 12/13/2001
Restricted Grant Purpose: Alterations and improvements to the South 8th Street Ministry Center.

I confirm that a grant in the amount stated above has been received by this organization. I further confirm that all the grant funds have been spent in accordance with the terms of the grant. The following is a financial breakdown and brief narrative on the use of the grant funds:

Also included is a statement indicating what impact the grant had on this organization. (Add separate page to provide more details, if necessary.)

Financial Breakdown:

- $17,000 paid to Stanley & Orke for repairs to the roof
- $1,000 paid for labor for tuckpointing holes, loose and cracked brick on exterior
- $1,000 paid for new insulation, 2 X 6's and ceiling tile for main upper room ceiling
- $400 paid for new doors and security
- $600 paid for interior renovations such as floor tiles, wall paint, bathroom fixture repair, and new carpet for room that had water damage prior to roof repair

Brief Narrative: Because the Center has been renovated enough to again be usable, the following are some of the activities that have recently been held in this building:

- Outreach to community men inviting them to watch NBA finals on a big screen in June of this year. As many as 15 adults and 12 teens came for the games.
- Monthly Saturday clubs for children. Volunteers came each month to play games with the children and teach them moral lessons.
- Summer Bible Camp. Volunteers joined the World Impact staff to hold a one week Bible Camp. World Impact staff canvassed the neighborhood with flyers for the camp. Forty children attended from over 19 different addresses in our community.
- Community Yard Sale—making donated goods available to the community at very reasonable prices. Clothing is 50 cents per pound and furniture and knickknacks are priced to sell. People from the community were also able to sell their own wares.
- One room is being used as a bedroom for a homeless man as he completes job-training programs and is mentored by a World Impact Staff member.

Each of these outreaches are part of a concerted effort to reach the African-American population of the surrounding community, with the desired end result being a self-supporting church ministering to the neighborhood. The repair of this building has impacted our organization by providing a site for all of these activities and the formation of a new team to work at this site.

This is a final report.

*Signature of Responsible Officer:*_____

Title: _____

Date: _____

The Hyde and Watson Foundation, 437 Southern Boulevard
  Chatham Township, NJ 07928 Tel. (973) 966-6024

These are presented as general models only. If a foundation supplies its own guidelines for reporting, then adhere to those instructions.

In sum, good practice when a grant has been awarded includes:

- say thank you
- convey excitement about your work and its success
- send requested materials, such as a signed grant contract, to the donor
- know what you are obligated to do
- get reports in on time
- communicate both positive and negative news to the grantmaker

Here is an example of a request to the William Bingham Foundation to reallocate grant funds received.

July 23, 2001

Ms. Laura H. Gilbertson, Director
The William Bingham Foundation
20325 Center Ridge Road, Suite 629
Rocky River, Ohio 44116

Dear Ms. Gilbertson:

In 1999 the William Bingham Foundation granted Fieldstone Farm Therapeutic Riding Center (TRC) $20,000 toward a list of several site development projects. Since then we have had several other foundations review our site needs and they have also helped to fund these projects. However, several of these other foundations have restricted their funding to particular items on our list. We ask that the William Bingham Foundation consider allowing Fieldstone Farm TRC to use $14,747 of the granted $20,000 to complete the funding need for the farm's parking lot paving which is a site development need that was not stated on the original proposal. Since your funding was restricted to capital projects we hope this will fit in with your interests.

Please contact me with any questions. Fieldstone Farm TRC is very appreciative of the support that the William Bingham Foundation has given. Thank you for your time and consideration.

Sincerely,

Lynnette Stuart
Executive Director

Seeking a Renewal

In certain cases, you will want to request that the grant be renewed or that a follow-up project be supported. Some funders refuse to give renewed support because they do not want to encourage dependency or because they see their funding as providing "seed money."

Other funders require a certain period of time to elapse between the grant and the renewal request. For instance, the Hearst Foundations currently require three years between grants.

Even a grant that could be a candidate for renewal may be labeled a one-time gift. Ordinarily the phrase "one-time gift" means that the funder is making no commitment to future funding. It does not necessarily mean that no possibility for future support exists.

If you know that you will want to request renewed support, you should communicate this early on to the foundation in order to determine the best time to submit another request. Be careful not to wait too long before requesting a renewal. By the time the funder receives the request, all the foundation's funds may be committed for the following year.

You should also determine early on the format required by the funder for submitting a renewal request. Some foundations require a full proposal; others want just a letter. This is another illustration of the differences among funders. It reinforces the need to communicate with the grantmaker to determine its particular requirements.

A report on funds expended and results of the first grant is a particularly critical document if you are going to ask for renewed support. However, many funders want your request for renewal to be separate from the report on the grant. In larger foundations, the report and the request for renewal might be handled by different departments; therefore, if you submit your renewal request as part of the report on the first grant, it might not find its way into the proposal system.

Following Up on a Declination

The most important response to a rejection letter is not to take it personally. An old fundraising adage is that "Campaigns fail because people don't ask, not because they get rejected." If your proposal gets rejected, it means you are out there asking. You are doing what you should be doing. Hopefully, you have sent your proposal to a number of other appropriate funders and have not put all your eggs in one basket. A rule of thumb is that you should approach three funders for every grant you need. Thus, even if one or two prospects turn your proposal down, you still have a shot at the third.

Some funders will talk with you about why the proposal was rejected, particularly if you had a meeting with the program staff at the granting institution prior to or at the time of submission. A phone call following a rejection letter can help you clarify the next step. Your request may have been of great interest to the foundation but was turned down in that funding cycle because the board had already committed all the funds set aside for projects in your subject or geographical area. For example, if your request was for an AIDS program in South Chicago, the foundation may have already committed its grants budget for that geographic area. A call to a foundation staff member might result in encouragement to reapply in a later funding cycle.

All funding representatives emphasize, however, the need to be courteous in the process of calling once you have received a rejection letter. It is never easy to say "no," and a program officer who fought hard for your proposal may feel almost as disappointed as you are that it was turned down. While foundation staff usually want to be helpful, it is important to recognize that it can often be difficult to tell someone why a proposal has been rejected.

Most of the grantmakers interviewed for this guide agree with Richard Jung of the Gill Foundation about the conversation that takes place after the declination. He said, "I often speak with organizations whose proposals have been declined, but they are not my favorite calls. It entails discussing with grantees the reasons why their grant was not funded. If they understand our decisions are not personal and are willing to listen to feedback, it can help them craft a better proposal next time—and then, we all win. While most turndowns are related to the foundation not having enough money, there are still many opportunities for a grantee to improve the overall proposal. So, if a grantee is persistent in seeking feedback and then incorporates those suggestions, their next proposal has a better chance of being supported. At our foundation, about fifty percent of grantees who follow this path eventually receive funding the next time around. It really does pay to get feedback."

It is important to take your cue from the funder, either from the rejection letter or from the follow-up call to staff. If you are not encouraged to resubmit, then you probably shouldn't.

There are times when a funder will encourage you to resubmit the same request at a particular time in the future. If you have been given this advice, then follow it. In your cover letter, be sure to refer to your conversation with the funding representative, remembering to restate, but not overstate, the earlier conversation.

Even if a foundation is not interested in funding the particular project you submitted, by keeping the lines of communication open and remaining respectful you will be nurturing the opportunity for future funding. Hildy Simmons, formerly of J.P. Morgan Private Bank, suggests, "Send a nice thank you letter. Indicate that you are disappointed but appreciate the process. Then keep us informed. And most importantly, don't take the rejection personally!"

In summary, best practice, when your request has been rejected, includes:

- say thank you
- figure out with the grantmaker what your next step should be
- follow the grantmaker's suggestions
- don't argue

What follows is a sample thank you following a rejection from Christ's Outreach for the Blind to the William Randolph Hearst Foundation.

April 17, 2003

Attention: Jackie
William Randolph Hearst Foundation
The Hearst Foundation, Inc.
888 Seventh Avenue
New York, NY 10106-0057

Dear Jackie:

Thank you so much for taking the time out of your busy schedule to talk with me concerning Christ's Outreach for the Blind's proposal dated February 24, 2003. I have to admit that I was disappointed, but with your explanation, I understand why we were declined. When we reach our million dollar budget (as long as we fall within Hearst Foundation Guidelines), we will be contacting you!

Again thank you for your consideration. Please keep us in your thoughts and prayers.

Respectfully,

April Harris, Office Manager

Final Tips

What to do if you receive a grant:

- Send a personalized thank you.
- Keep the funder informed of your progress.
- Follow the funder's reporting requirements.

What to do if your request is turned down:

- Don't take it personally.
- Be sure you understand why.
- Find out if you can resubmit at a later date.

13

What the Funders Have to Say

Our conversations with the 40 grantmakers we interviewed were rich, insightful, and enjoyable. To make some sense out of the diversity of commentary we gathered and the various opinions expressed, in this summary we will address three overarching themes: the proposal submission and review process itself, including the document and decision making; technological innovations; and perceived trends impacting foundations.

The proposal submission and review process

You may well be reading this chapter hoping to find the silver bullet that will ensure your next foundation or corporate grant. While this may be disappointing news for some, the grantmakers we talked to are quite consistent in stating that in fact there is no one magic formula. Rather, they recommend a holistic approach to thinking and strategizing about the proposal-writing process. They agree that the most important steps to take are also the most obvious: Follow the funder's guidelines and continue to cultivate and reach out to those that support you and those that are not yet donors.

Be certain to do your research thoroughly before any contact with the funder. Any conversation with a funder will be more conclusive and lead to specific next steps if you have conducted the necessary homework in advance. Be persistent in cultivation of likely candidates to support your organization. Don't take it personally if your proposal is declined the first or even second or third time you submit it. And, though this may seem obvious, be sure to include the amount you need in the cover letter, and send a thank-you note when you receive a grant. Strive constantly to improve on your writing, and view the process as a continuous learning experience. It is critical to always keep the lines of communication open with prospective and current funders on your list.

In general the foundation and corporate grantmaking representatives we spoke with are satisfied with the components of a grant proposal and elements of the proposal package as they are presented in this book and its earlier editions.

The grantmakers we interviewed for this edition, in particular, portray themselves as highly engaged with the nonprofit organizations they ultimately fund in all stages of the application process. They express a willingness to speak on the phone with grantseekers about a proposed application. A number of them describe being intimately involved in the actual design of the grant project. They explain that it is very important to them to see a real relationship develop between the grantmaker and the nonprofit grantee. Elan Garonzik of the Charles Stewart Mott Foundation, for example, insists that this relationship is *the* important part of the grant application and proposal process. Those we interviewed emphasized the critical nature of the grantmaker/grantee relationship much more than in prior years. These grantmakers underscore their desire to enter into a partnership with nonprofits they support in tough times as well as in good times.

Today's grantmakers are sharpening their internal review process as they perform "due diligence" concerning grant applications. A critical step for most involves sitting down face to face with grant applicants or even making a site visit to a nonprofit organization, especially one not previously funded by them. The majority of our interviewees acknowledge that it takes a significant amount of time to prepare for such a meeting, but they deem it important to do. In the course of site visits or other meetings grantmakers expect to discern a sense of continuity between the picture that emerges from the proposal narrative and what they actually observe when they talk to representatives of the grantseeking organization.

While a proposal is under review grantmakers urge applicants to stay in touch with them. Virtually all of our interviewees felt calls or written communication to provide updates, news of funding received, possible enhancements to the project, or changes within the organization's leadership were very appropriate and consistent with the grantmaker's desire to play an active role in the project design.

Nearly half of the interviewees also suggested that communication at this stage between a board member from the grantseeking organization and a board member of the foundation was acceptable. They caution, however, that it is important to let grantmaking staff know that that contact is taking place.

Because in the last few years grantmakers have been attempting to do more with less, they tend to skip the letter of intent phase of the application process. Many interviewees note that the letter of intent can help the grantmaker understand the request before the nonprofit organization goes to all the effort of submitting a complete proposal. But they go on to say that currently they simply do not have the staff or time to review both documents. Clearly this is a temporary and short-term solution to the pressures that grantmakers currently face.

For nonprofits competing for scarce grant dollars, particularly those whose financial sustainability is marginal, mergers seem to be high on the list of solutions grantmakers encourage those with compatible missions to consider. At the same time collaborations as a strategy to survive are less popular than in previous years, unless they make real economic sense. Several of our grantmakers reported that forced collaborations, dictated by the funder or the nonprofit's board, are often undertaken halfheartedly. They may have minimal impact, while generating a big drain on staff resources.

The grantmakers we interviewed continue to make themselves available to speak with the representative of a nonprofit even after a proposal has been rejected. Most confess that they do not personally like these conversations, but they agree that the applicant has a right to inquire about next steps. They reminded us that the reason behind most declinations is simply inadequate grant money to satisfy the demand. Thus a request that fits a grantmaker's guidelines and is well presented can still be turned down due to lack of funds. Yet there still seems to be hope for those who are persistent, since most of our interviewees indicate that a resubmitted application the following year or grant cycle, especially from those invited to resubmit, stands a much better chance of being funded. It is a commonly accepted tenet of fundraising that sometimes you need to ask two or three times before you hear a "yes."

Ensuring that grantees report back to the grantmaker at the culmination of a grant project continues to be a very high priority item for our funders. The preponderance of our interviewees note that to ensure that applicants are fully aware in advance of what will be expected of them, reporting requirements are described in detail on their Web sites or in their award letters. When it comes to the evaluation section of the proposal, our grantmakers suggest being very realistic about what can be accomplished and reasonable about what can be measured. They require enough data to fully appreciate the project's specific objectives, but they realize that some applicants may not be sophisticated about how to design an effective evaluation of the impact of a grant. Many expressed a willingness to help with this aspect of reporting back to them.

Beyond the basic components of the proposal document, funders look for solid financial information about the project and about the agency. Those we interviewed are particularly interested in who else is or might be supporting the project. They want a short, concise narrative with a minimum number of attachments. And it is obvious from the many conversations we held that grantmakers are frustrated by incomplete applications, which then slow their review process.

When asked about their approach to actually reading a proposal, the majority of our grantmakers admit to skipping around the document rather than reading from beginning to end. Three sections of the proposal package continue to be those looked at first: the cover letter, the executive summary, and the budget. And subsequently the proposal reviewers say they then pay special attention to the project description and the section on financial sustainability.

Our interviewees prefer a proposal package that is error-free and simply put together with no binders or other fancy trappings.

Technological innovations

Conversations we held with grantmakers about technology were very lively and informative. The majority we interviewed deem themselves technologically savvy and are convinced that technology has a key role to play in facilitating the proposal process. This is a significant change from what we reported in prior editions of this guide. Today's grantmakers are pleased with the impact the Web has made on their own operations and that of grantseekers.

Most of our interviewees do have a Web site that includes their guidelines and a list of grants awarded. They observe that the Web seems to makes the grant applicant's prospect research efforts much easier. They speak glowingly of raising the levels of communication on both sides of the grantmaking equation, because grantseekers can use the Internet to find the information they need so much more easily than in the past.

Most of the grantmakers we interviewed report that they use e-mail a great deal of the time to communicate with applicants and grantees. This is also a relatively new development and differs from what we were told for prior editions of this guide. They use it to request additional data during the proposal review process and even to stay up to date on projects they have already funded. The interviewees state that they are pleased with the speed and convenience that e-mail offers. Of course, the continuing need to print out copies of certain e-mails for record retention purposes is often mentioned as well.

Nonetheless, the acceptance of e-mail technology in the day-to-day workplace does not necessarily translate to accepting applications electronically. The primary stumbling block seems to be the need for certain attachments (like the IRS tax-exempt designation letter or financial audit), which most of our interviewees require, and which cannot yet be submitted electronically. If the proposal is sent via e-mail and hard copies of the attachments sent via snail mail, it is the grantmaker who winds up with responsibility for assembling the application package. And if multiple copies of proposals are required for review by trustees who are not yet fully utilizing e-mail, again it is the grantmaker who has to print out the copies. Most do not have adequate staff to handle that level of detail. And while a slightly greater number of foundations now accept proposals submitted entirely online (and a few—though not those we interviewed—*only* accept proposals that way), most do not have online application forms at their Web sites as yet. So the requirement still exists at most foundations to submit the final proposal the old-fashioned way, by mail.

Our grantmakers had a few suggestions for applicants utilizing e-mail and other technology. They caution against asking multiple questions via e-mail. Second, as with any proposals, those submitting their application electronically should not wait until the very last minute to apply. And they should be sure to send the proposal to the correct e-mail address. Finally, "broadcast" e-mailings to grantmakers, just like other mass mailings, are, of course, a waste of time.

Embracing technology as an adjunct to their daily work is something relatively new to grantmakers. Those we spoke with seem to be doing so with great enthusiasm.

Trends impacting grantmaking

When the prior edition of this guide was issued, grantmakers were enjoying unprecedented financial strength. Today they are working very hard to recover from a recent significant economic downturn. Looking at the last decade as a whole, many of our grantmakers saw real growth in their assets. Yet by the time we conducted these interviews, assets were down, in some cases significantly, against the market highs of the year 2000. Each grantmaker we asked about this had a unique response to the (hopefully) short-term loss of assets. Their proposed remedies tended to fall into one of two categories: (1) staff reductions and (2) refocusing of grants. Actually giving away far less money was mentioned by only a few.

The first strategy is fairly straightforward, since it amounts to simple, albeit painful, belt-tightening. Christine Park of Lucent Technologies neatly describes the shift as, ". . . downsizing of staff and upsizing of responsibility." Most grantmakers we talked to prefer to trim their own costs before making substantial cuts to their grants budgets. Several CEOs at staffed foundations that we spoke with did express concern about the potential strain this approach places on the remaining program officers whose positions have not been eliminated.

The discussion of "refocusing" of grants was much more far ranging. A few of our interviewees admitted to having strayed just a bit from strict adherence to published grantmaking guidelines in the years when funds were plentiful. Today these grantmakers are carefully redirecting awards to only those who meet the guidelines in every sense, with no exceptions. Quite a few foundations determine their grants budgets based on a rolling average of three to five years, and this has served somewhat to blunt the impact of asset losses they may have suffered. And, yes, there are some who have actually reduced grants amounts and eliminated recipients. These grantmakers talked about struggling with several alternatives: funding only existing grantees, making cuts in grants size across the board to all recipients, limiting funding to already strong institutions, or not supporting start-ups. In general, though, most grantmakers we spoke to remain optimistic about their ability to weather financial hard times and still get their job of giving away money done well.

Several of our interviewees alluded to the fact that philanthropy itself is experiencing a sea change. Old paradigms no longer pertain. Philanthropy, once regarded as benevolent charity, is now seen by many as a social investment. Foundations that used to be called upon to start projects that were then taken over by government funding sources are now somehow expected to pick up the slack when public funding is no longer there. Meanwhile, a lot of attention is being paid to how foundations are run, what percentage of their assets they pay out each year, what administrative costs are allowable, and if and how much they pay their trustees. The grantmakers we talked to cite a compelling need to become "transparent," accountable, and less standoffish. At the same time these grantmakers believe that the public, the media, and especially Congress need a better understanding of how foundations operate. A great deal is going on behind the scenes, and that includes government scrutiny.

Throughout it all, these remarkable grantmakers remain upbeat, positive, and highly engaged. As Karen Rosa of the Altman Foundation says, "It is our job to help nonprofits succeed." And Bruce Esterline of the Meadows Foundation states, "There is a joy and magic to this business."

What follows are selected responses to our questions in the grantmakers' own words. Other responses will be found throughout the remaining chapters as quotes we've selected to exemplify key points being made.

Do you find that most grantseekers have done their homework before contacting you?

Most are prepared when they come to us, but we're doing our part to inform them also. (Peter Bird)

Research is key. We encourage grantseekers to refer to our Web site and specifically look at the grants we made before applying. We don't get a lot of requests outside of our areas of interest, but many that come in are still very broad in scope. (Robert Crane)

More than ever before. (Joseph S. Dolan)

More are doing their homework. We get people calling for guidelines, and then some of them do follow up. Those who call with substantive questions show that they have taken an initial look at who we are. (William V. Engel)

We work with nonprofits to help determine their eligibility. (Roxanne Ford)

Most nonprofits do their research. The ones that don't stand out. (P. Russell Hardin)

People seem to know a lot about us—and that's great. (Ruby Lerner)

Our Web site has helped a lot—[it's made] a huge difference, in fact. Callers are now more informed. (Maria Mottola)

Applicants are far more knowledgeable. (David Odahowski)

Those who do not do due diligence are taking a stab in the dark and are potentially wasting their limited fundraising resources. (Christine Park)

Grantseekers now take time not only to read our guidelines but also to look at sample grants, to find out whom we fund. (Karen Rosa)

For the most part, nonprofits are doing more and more research, including visiting our Web site. As grantmakers we are trying to be clear about what we do. It is not in our best interest to be inundated with proposals that have no chance of funding. (Mary Beth Salerno)

What is the best initial approach to your foundation?

The telephone call is the most effective communication vehicle to get to the proposal stage. Call up and let's talk. (Peter Bird)

Fifty to seventy-five percent of applications are preceded by conversations. It works better to have a level of engagement—sometimes one or more calls—before a proposal is submitted. (David K. Gibbs)

A call or e-mail to start is fine. (P. Russell Hardin)

We have an open door policy—especially in the pre-proposal stage. (Marci Lu)

If we have funded an organization before, we are happy to receive a letter of intent about a project and why our support is needed. (Maria Mottola)

I want a letter of intent. I like to see it in writing. (Mary Beth Salerno)

After a quick call or e-mail, I am inclined to request a letter of intent before inviting the complete proposal document. (Hildy Simmons)

Some simple questions about the proposal process can be answered on e-mail. (Elizabeth Smith)

I find the letter of intent to be unnecessary—[it involves] extra reading and steps. (E. Belvin Williams)

We are open and accessible, so a phone call to start is fine. (Nancy Wiltsek)

How do you usually read a grant request?

First, I go to the project section. I want to be excited about the project. Then I look at who else is supporting the project and the organization. I check the finances. Are they healthy? Finally I look at the board list. I want to see who the people are who will make the organization hum. (Hunter Corbin)

I can get a great deal out of a review of the budget. (David K. Gibbs)

First, I look at the project section. That is what we are looking to support. Then I go to the budgets and compare the project narrative with the budget. I care about the project, yes, but about the organization as well. I want to know: Is the project fiscally sound?
(Laura H. Gilbertson)

I read the executive summary first. It should be succinct, not flowery. It should tell me what the program is and why it is needed.
(Mary Gregory)

The financial statements are important. They provide a real look at the agency: how they spend their resources; where the resources came from; who sustains the organization. (P. Russell Hardin)

I find the cover letter to be very helpful. I hope it will direct me to what the agency is looking for. Also, it should tell me: Did we fund them before? (J. Andrew Lark)

First, I love a good executive summary. It should tell me: what you need, how you will implement the project, what you do as an organization. You should be able to say it all in two pages. (Ilene Mack)

The cover letter makes a difference. It should tell me who wants this to happen, what is the story and why and how. (Maria Mottola)

The budget and agency financial documents, if clear and concise, provide a great deal of information about the nonprofit. I learn quickly about how meaningful the request is. (David Odahowski)

Make your case in the cover letter and executive summary. Then give the detail after that. I need to find information quickly.
(Christine Park)

The request section is the guts of the document. What will you use the money for? [The] level of detail is important. I am disappointed when there is not enough detail, such as: what is this organization or project about, how does it work, how many people will it serve, what are projected outcomes? Don't assume we know. (Elizabeth Smith)

It depends on how thick it is. I want to read from beginning to end but skip around when the document is too large. Be concise. Describe how the project fits the grantmaker's mission. I want to find out: what the problem is, what they will do about it, is it sustainable? (David O. Egner)

Does your foundation/corporation acknowledge in writing all proposals it receives?

Yes, we acknowledge receipt in writing, but a proposal submitted after our deadline may sit for a couple of months before the applicant hears back from the foundation. (Hunter Corbin)

We will be in touch within 30 to 60 days, but we do not communicate in writing. We will discuss with the grantee why the proposal was rejected or what to expect next. (David O. Egner)

Thirty-six hours is the goal for an acknowledgement to be sent. (Bruce Esterline)

Within a couple of days of receipt, we will communicate in writing either a declination or: 1) the need for additional information, 2) when the project will be considered, 3) if we wish to arrange a visit. (P. Russell Hardin)

Yes, we acknowledge proposals in writing, but we will also call some of our prospective grantees. (Christine Park)

Yes, we send a postcard. (Mary Beth Salerno)

Yes, we customarily send e-mail notices acknowledging receipt of all proposals. (Jeff Schwartz)

Yes, the grantseeker will hear from us within one week.
(Nancy Wiltsek)

How long does the process of review typically take at your foundation/corporation?

Our review process is three to four months long. A project will sit longer if we are waiting for information or for other grantmakers to award a gift. (Bruce Esterline)

We take three to four months to review a request. (Larry Kressley)

Three to four months. First the proposal is logged in. Staff meets monthly for a preliminary review. Then the board grants committee looks at the application, followed by a full board review.
(Hunter Corbin)

Our process takes three to six months. It includes the following: The proposal is logged in and the application is acknowledged within a week of receipt. When we have all of the documentation, we read the full request. Then we do a site visit because we want to see the program in action. (Nancy Wiltsek)

Once a proposal is pending, is it okay for the grantseeker to call you to check on the status of the request or to share information? Is it okay to send additional materials?

If we need more information, the foundation will ask, but it is okay to communicate significant changes. (Joseph S. Dolan)

If there is new data and information pertinent to the project, we want to hear about it. But don't overdo. Excessive persistence might yield negative results. (Roxanne Ford)

We definitely want to see or hear information that would change the nature of the application or impact what is proposed. We are building trust at this stage, which bodes well for the relationship.
(David K. Gibbs)

Not at the letter of intent stage, but once the proposal is submitted, we welcome this information. We especially like to see updates on fundraising successes. (Laura H. Gilbertson and Elizabeth B. Meers)

Bits of important information are welcome, if they will enhance my understanding of the program, or if it's news about other funding—grants received or grants *not* received. (Mary Gregory)

It is essential that we know what's up. We want to get regular updates. (Larry Kressley)

It couldn't hurt, especially to share news of a new grant to the project. If staff has changed, let us know. People are reluctant to share bad news. It is refreshing to get bad news in advance to alert us to the unexpected. (J. Andrew Lark)

We appreciate newsworthy updates. Pertinent information helps strengthen the case, especially if other anticipated funding comes through. (Marci Lu)

Squeaky wheels get the oil. Don't be a pest, however, and show up too frequently. This is a dynamic process, not a static one. (David Odahowski)

There is a fine line between due diligence and pressure. (Christine Park)

Communicate what you want us to know, but do so concisely. Check with your program officer if there is a question. (Jeff Schwartz)

Should grantseekers check in on the process? No, unless they have other information to share that is relevant to the request. (Elizabeth Smith)

Is it all right if a board member from the nonprofit organization contacts one of your board members directly?

I don't mind. It does happen. (Hunter Corbin)

It won't help here. The board prefers not to be approached by potential grantseekers. With many foundations, however, it is helpful to have a board contact. (Robert Crane)

It happens all the time that board-to-board contact is made. When my board members are contacted, they will call the program officer and let the staff run with it. (Jim DeNova)

I have no problem with this. It can help me if I want board support. But give our staff a heads-up that this contact is going to take place. (David O. Egner)

This is a free country. If you have a personal relationship, talk to that individual. The board of our foundation respects the board/staff relationship. Board members say: "Use the process. I'm only one vote, anyway." (Bruce Esterline)

Applicants do ask us up front about this. Organizations consider board contact an advantage. They may use their contacts, but we appreciate it when they let us know about it. Educate the trustees, don't pressure them. (Roxanne Ford)

It could be a plus to our due diligence. (David K. Gibbs)

It doesn't matter, and this hardly ever happens. (David Grant and Cynthia Evans)

I've never had a problem with this, but I'd prefer if you told me first. I'll provide good guidance. Be upfront about it. I will try to help. (Ilene Mack)

This is a touchy issue. If you know someone, it doesn't hurt to reach out to that person. But the proposal should stand on its own merits. A proposal that can't fly without help causes a difficult situation. Don't do an end-run around staff. (Karen Rosa)

The proposal should stand on its merit—not its influence. (Ruth Shack)

Do you expect reports/evaluations from grantees? Do you remind a grantee when you expect the reports/evaluations to be submitted?

We like to see an evaluation section in the proposal. Otherwise, how will the nonprofit determine if the project is working? Within three months of the conclusion of a grant, the Trustees review a summary of the project. They are learning from experience what does and does not work. We seldom use an outside evaluator. (Laura H. Gilbertson and Elizabeth B. Meers)

Our grant reporting form is designed to serve as a valuable learning tool for both foundation staff and grantees. We greatly appreciate a candid, thoughtful review of the project experience. (Marci Lu)

In the proposal, articulate that you will send reports. Tell me their timing, frequency, and that you will share successes and challenges. (Christine Park)

There is a lack of knowledge about how to evaluate.
(E. Belvin Williams)

They have to tell us how they spent the money. Otherwise, the organization is not eligible for future grants. The reports don't have to be elaborate. (Hunter Corbin)

We expect reports three months after completion of a one-year grant; interim reports are due each year of multi-year grants. We will follow up if the report is late. We do not use external evaluators except in rare circumstances. (Robert Crane)

During the review process we tell grantees when reports are due. We want to know how close they came to achieving a goal. We do not use evaluators. (David O. Egner)

In the report we want to know what was anticipated, what happened, and what was the mid-course adjustment. (David K. Gibbs)

A grantmaker shouldn't use the report to penalize the grantee. The report should help both the grantmaker and the grantee figure out how to build capacity and how to get feedback on the work they are doing, because assessment improves the quality of the work. (David Grant and Cynthia Evans)

Reporting sometimes falls through the cracks. We don't close the file until we get a written report. Our emphasis is on results.
(P. Russell Hardin)

A nonprofit will not be re-granted without submitting a report on progress. (Richard Jung)

Our award letter clearly states when reports are due and includes a reporting form. (Marci Lu)

We want to know what happened. Reports should educate the grant-maker about the issue—while not being preachy, pedantic, or patronizing. (Elspeth Revere)

The transmittal letter indicates when reports are due. We are work-ing to have more effective reporting forms and to help grantees think about their impact from the beginning of the project. It is critical that grantmakers use reports from nonprofits to help both sides understand how well they are doing and the impact of the grant dollars. (Karen Rosa)

I need clarity, not reams of paper. How have things gone? How did you use the money? Did it match up with the original request? (Hildy Simmons)

Following the rejection of an application, do you speak with the applicant about the declination if they ask you to?

It is good to talk about the rejection. We will be blunt about our con-cerns. (Peter Bird)

Yes, I am willing to have this conversation. I turn the discussion into an instructive opportunity. (David K. Gibbs)

Our board member who is the nonprofit's contact will call and explain the rejection as well as discuss next steps. (Laura H. Gilbertson and Elizabeth B. Meers)

Absolutely. I will have this conversation although it is not my favorite thing to do. Usually a nonprofit is turned down due to a lack of money. It is important to know that, most of the time, it is not the nonprofit's fault that it was turned down. (Mary Gregory)

I encourage this. A program officer will speak to applicants within ten days of their call requesting additional information.
(Larry Kressley)

Absolutely, since the nonprofit has a right to this conversation. We suggest what to do next and if possible other grantmakers to approach. (Ilene Mack)

The rejection letter is very generic. A program officer will call and talk with the applicant about the turndown. (Rebecca Martin)

We try to be specific about why we turned a proposal down. The hardest calls to make are in this climate when lack of money is the only reason for the rejection. (Maria Mottla)

I am absolutely willing to have this conversation. It is part of my job. Often I go back into the file and re-read our notes in order to give appropriate feedback. Sometimes I will hang onto a promising proposal that we couldn't fund, in case I can help at another time. (Christine Park)

This is still the hardest thing for me after 12 years in grantmaking. (Elspeth Revere)

Absolutely—we are open and accessible when it comes to discussing rejections. I will be as honest as possible. Sometimes there is nothing the organization can do. It was beyond their control. (Nancy Wiltsek)

What is the best thing an organization can do after being turned down?

Accept it. Understand why. Move on. (A. Thomas Hildebrandt)

If you don't know why you were rejected, call and politely probe. If you know why, don't call; it is not helpful. Send a thank you letter for the grantmaker's time and consideration. (J. Andrew Lark)

Don't burn your bridges. (David Odahowski)

If there is a fit, try again. Use common sense—don't kid yourself. Be realistic. (Mary Beth Salerno)

Use good manners: Say thank you for the consideration. Ask to meet, but don't badger us on the phone. Come back if appropriate. (E. Belvin Williams)

Call the program officer, especially if you had a relationship. Get a clear understanding of why you were turned down.
(Eugene R. Wilson)

What is the worst thing an organization can do after being turned down?

Send the same proposal over and over again. (Robert Crane)

Challenge the foundation's priorities and mission—thinking that somehow we will change our priorities. (Jim DeNova)

Go to my board and tell them I am dumb for turning you down. (David O. Egner)

Take it personally. (A. Thomas Hildebrandt)

Try to "appeal" the process. Say that you want to take it to our board! (Larry Kressley)

Call up and be angry. A turndown is never personal. There are always good reasons. Unprofessional behavior is counterproductive. (Ilene Mack)

Don't be demoralized. A rejection is not a stain on one's reputation. (John E. Marshall, III)

From the organization's standpoint, the worst thing would be to go away and never come back without learning what, if anything, could have been done to write a winning proposal. (Jeff Schwartz)

Send an annoying letter; be angry; call us stupid. (Hildy Simmons)

If a grant is awarded, what is the best thing an organization can do?

Say thank you. We share many of these letters with the board and family. Get reports in on time. Keep sending information beyond the grant period. We are always happy to see beyond the "snapshot" of the grant. Cultivate us—via phone and/or mail. We want a partnership that is ongoing. (Bruce Esterline)

Stay in communication; don't disappear until you need money again. (David Ford)

Send a thank you letter that we can share with our directors. (Roxanne Ford)

Share information about the award strategically, as relevant. (Elan Garonzik)

Review the proposal and know what you are obligated to do. Do what you can do to fulfill the agreement in good faith. Update and communicate with us along the way. Call after the grant was awarded to touch base and to discuss reports. (David K. Gibbs)

Send a personal letter to say thank you. Convey excitement about your work and its success. (David Grant and Cynthia Evans)

Complete the project successfully and report the impact of the grant to the foundation. (P. Russell Hardin)

Say thank you. Just a quick acknowledgement or nice phone call is all that's required. If the project does not go forward, talk to us about it. (A. Thomas Hildebrandt)

Communicate often with program staff. Follow the grant requirements. If there is a problem, be forthright with the program officer, so that together creative solutions can be worked out and the project can be successful. (Rebecca Martin)

Keep us informed—this shouldn't be too much of a burden. (Eugene R. Wilson)

If a grant is awarded, what is the worst thing an organization can do?

Take the money and run. Then we hear from them again only when they need more money. (Peter Bird)

Not use the funds well. Be deceptive about the money or about the evaluation. (Robert Crane)

Not reply at all. (In such a case, the applicant probably would not be funded again). (William V. Engel)

Send no thank you or report. Even worse, and a mistake with long-lasting consequences for future grants, is for an organization to mis-construe or misrepresent the grant. (Roxanne Ford)

Make changes in program or budget without telling us. In most cases a grant is restricted to what was described in the proposal. We don't like to find out about changes so late in the game. The grantee really should have gotten permission in advance. Spending the money on unapproved activities is also a mistake. (Laura H. Gilbertson and Elizabeth B. Meers)

Not even sending a letter confirming that they got the check. (Mary Gregory)

Fail to capitalize on the opportunity. (P. Russell Hardin)

Call and say "why didn't you give me as much as I asked for?" (David Palenchar)

Beyond the basic information, should the proposal's cover letter contain any other data?

The cover letter should be short, succinct, and direct.
(P. Russell Hardin)

I prefer that the letter not exceed two pages. (Laura H. Gilbertson)

I like to see a summary of the project in the cover letter.
(David O. Egner)

The cover letter should include the grant start and end dates.
(Ruth Shack)

Tell us how much you are asking us to give in a one-year and/or multi-year period. Make this clear. (Elizabeth Smith)

Provide a general statement about what the proposed program will achieve. (Nancy Wiltsek)

Who should sign the cover letter?

It is good policy to have the CEO sign the cover letter.
(William V. Engel)

The cover letter should be signed by the person ultimately responsible for signing grant contracts on behalf of the applicant. For renewals, Mott accepts letters signed by the project leader. But in all cases the grant agreement has to be signed by an individual authorized to enter into contract on behalf of the grantee organization.
(Elan Garonzik)

The CEO or a senior administrative official should sign the cover letter. (John E. Marshall, III)

It really doesn't matter to us, but it makes the most sense to have the person who will be our contact sign the cover letter. (Mary Gregory)

Beyond the basic information, should the proposal contain any other data?

Within the statement of need and project description, we look for the following: the target population or community to be served, strategies for implementing the work, a timetable for achieving outcomes, and a plan for continuing the work beyond the grant period, if appropriate. (Robert Crane)

I want to see the logical flow of information from one section of the proposal to the next. (David O. Egner)

Information that will help me understand how you will keep the project going after the funding period. (Marci Lu)

Make clear what is the relevance of your project to our foundation's objectives. (Rebecca Martin)

An explanation of why the grantmaker is considered an appropriate donor for the project. (Elspeth Revere)

Discuss the organization's capacity to undertake the project. (Ruth Shack)

A timetable showing the implementation of the project can be helpful. (Larry Kressley)

Beyond the basic information, should the appendix contain any other data?

Additional information about your agency's donors, including: a list of the five current, largest funders; a list of the five largest funders during the last five years; and cumulative grant totals for each year. (Robert Crane)

A list of grantmakers with whom your proposal is pending is helpful. (Joseph S. Dolan)

Please remember to give us the IRS Letter of Determination, not your sales tax exemption. (William V. Engel)

I like to see an organization chart. (Laura H. Gilbertson)

In the appendix there should be a statement that notes that the grant request has been approved by the applicant's governing body. (David Palenchar)

As proposal attachments, do you find brochures, videos, newspaper clippings, anecdotal information, and/or endorsements useful?

Ask us, if you have something you want to send and we haven't specified it in our guidelines. (David O. Egner)

Nonprofit organizations usually send too much extra material. (William V. Engel)

We discourage agencies from sending their videos. (Elan Garonzik)

We really don't want to see videos. (P. Russell Hardin)

Supplemental materials should be held to a minimum. Video tapes should not be sent unless specifically requested. (Ilene Mack)

If you send newspaper clippings, keep the number down to three recent articles. (Maria Mottola)

Can you share any specific feedback about the physical presentation of a proposal?

Make the document concise. Make it "user friendly."
(Christine Park)

Include all that we ask for in our application guidelines. Try to have the package complete. Having to request and wait for missing documents slows down our review of your proposal. (Karen Rosa)

Think about the credibility of your proposal package. If there are mistakes and errors, it doesn't look good. You should have taken the time to proof the document carefully. Budgets that do not add up are a problem. (Elan Garonzik)

If the proposal package is sloppy, it makes me think the agency is not well run. (Hunter Corbin)

Content is more important than the package. (David O. Egner)

There are no points given for format or packaging; we don't value form over substance. (P. Russell Hardin)

In a close decision, sloppiness does make the difference. Please proofread! (William V. Engel)

Take the binder or cover off the document. (David Grant, Cynthia Evans)

Do not bind the document. (John E. Marshall, III)

Does your foundation/corporation have a Web site?

Our Web site has been the catalyst for more and better applications. (Bruce Esterline)

We have a Web site, and it has made a big difference. (John E. Marshall, III)

Our Web site was a valuable investment. We are able to disseminate information very quickly. Applicants are knowledgeable about who we are and what we fund. (David Odahowski)

Our Web site provides electronic access to helpful application guidelines and vital programmatic priorities. (Rebecca Martin)

We are taking great pains to improve our Web site. Referring to it minimizes the time investment for the grantee and for staff. (Eugene R. Wilson)

Our Web site has been a positive experience for us. It increases access to and transparency of the foundation. (Larry Kressley)

It is very interesting having a Web site. Requests for information have actually dropped off. Grantseekers go to the Web site to get data, and going online is faster for grantseekers and not so costly. They seem to follow our instructions fairly well. (E. Belvin Williams)

Do you use e-mail to communicate with grantseekers?

We use e-mail to gather additional information during the proposal review stage, as well as to see what is happening after a grant has been awarded. (Peter Bird)

E-mail is simpler than faxing! We use it a lot to request and gather information. (David K. Gibbs)

This has dramatically changed our work! (Mary Gregory)

You can handle short, easy questions on e-mail. If a piece of information is needed and is not complicated or many pages, then e-mail is okay. (Ilene Mack)

We are using e-mail more and more. The upside is that it is fast. The downside is that you lose "something" in the transmission. You don't get the some feeling that you do from a call or a meeting. (David Odahowski)

I keep hard copies of all e-mails. (Christine Park)

Does your foundation/corporation accept proposals electronically?

Submitting a proposal online is not usually an advantage at our foundation unless time is of the essence. If we receive a proposal online, we end up having to print out the narrative and assemble the attachments. This is an extra step and we don't have a huge staff. (Robert Crane)

We don't accept proposals online but are working on it. First we need a secure place on our Web site for our board so that we can share proposal data with them electronically. (Roxanne Ford)

I like to have a hard copy in the file. (Mary Gregory)

We want the supporting documentation at the same time as the proposal narrative. So for now, it is easier to send the proposal by regular mail. (P. Russell Hardin)

A nonprofit can e-mail the proposal, but the supporting documents have to go in the mail. (Richard Jung)

We want a hard copy. Life doesn't have to be quite so fast. (Ilene Mack)

We simply don't have the staff capacity to do this. (Ruth Shack)

Submitting proposals electronically is not an effective way to make anyone's work easier, due to the myriad attachments. It's easier to mail the whole thing in. (Hildy Simmons)

What makes a grantseeker competitive?

1. Make a good presentation

Do your *research*. Have a sense of what issues the grantmaker is interested in and the criteria for awarding grants. (Robert Crane)

Probe deeply into a foundation. Learn how they measure effectiveness. Understand their expectations for themselves. Know who is responsible for them. Understand that this is not a homogeneous industry; all grantmakers are not alike. (Jim DeNova)

Learn the personality of the funder. (J. Andrew Lark)

2. Build a relationship with the grantmaker

Work on establishing good communication with staff. The more the staff knows, the more likely the outcome will be positive. (Roxanne Ford)

Build relationships. They will pay off. (Ilene Mack)

Really work to get "face time" with the staff. It really makes a difference. (Christine Park)

Build a relationship with trust with your program officer. Understand what the foundation is trying to accomplish. Make sure that your organization's proposal is aligned with the mission and priorities of the foundation. (Jeff Schwartz)

It's also about the relationship, not just the written word. (Elan Garonzik)

3. *Give us what we ask for*

Read the guidelines. (William V. Engel).

Pay attention to instructions so that what we asked for is included. (Ruby Lerner)

Take the risk of being honest with the grantmaker. (Nancy Wiltsek)

4. *Think beyond the moment*

Take the long view. (John E. Marshall, III)

Organizations need to be engaged in conversations about collaboration and mergers. (Richard Jung)

Broaden your base of support by expanding the variety of your funding sources. (Rebecca Martin)

Build a learning culture. Change is constant, so be able and ready to adapt. (Jeff Schwartz)

You need to build in time to think, to handle unexpected technological problems, and to bridge transition among staff. (Elan Garonzik)

What trends are you seeing?

1. That this is a period of transition handled differently by different grantmakers

We have had a decline in our assets. However, over the long term we experienced real growth. (Ruth Shack)

Our assets are down somewhat. Over time I expect that they will come back. We fund based on a five-year rolling average, so grants are not greatly affected. (J. Andrew Lark)

I am hearing that some portfolios are down 15–50%. Each grant-maker responds in an individual manner. (Hunter Corbin)

We are refocusing how we spend dollars. (Jim DeNova)

There are constraints on most foundation budgets, and increased needs and expectations. I don't believe we've seen the end of that cycle yet. (Robert Crane)

Nonprofits are operating in an entirely different environment. They face diminished resources and growing needs.
(P. Russell Hardin)

Private philanthropy cannot make up for the loss of public funding being experienced by many nonprofits. (Marci Lu)

Although our assets have declined, we've kept our grants budget steady, or slightly up. Our trustees are committed to doing more in difficult times. (Penelope McPhee)

When our assets were greater, we may have gotten slightly out of focus in our grant giving. We have to shape up now, since we have fewer dollars, and we have to achieve more with less. (Eugene R. Wilson)

Our foundation is doing more with fewer program and administrative staff. We are adapting to the circumstances.
(Bruce Esterline)

We are experiencing downsizing of staff and upsizing of responsibility. (Christine Park)

I am concerned about the program officers at foundations. They are worried about budget cuts. They are terribly busy. They are absorbing incredible change. So many are depending on them. People go into this business for a reason. Today's environment is depressing to many of them. (Penelope McPhee)

2. *That philanthropy is experiencing a sea change*

There is a change in how philanthropy is viewed and in how it perceives itself, from one of benevolent charity to social investment. This changes the strategy of giving. (Jim DeNova)

It used to be that philanthropy would start a project and then government would step in and provide the ongoing support, but not anymore. This changes how we think about grantmaking. (David O. Egner)

We have to humanize the role of the grantmaker in an era of outcomes. (Nancy Wiltsek)

Grantmakers must become more transparent and accountable. We need to talk to one another more. (Ilene Mack)

The old paradigms of traditional grantmaking must change. The new grantmaker needs to respond to a community's need and to cultural relevance. (Rebecca Martin)

3. *That philanthropy is under scrutiny.*

The role of philanthropy in general is under scrutiny. (Jeff Schwartz)

We are worried that the tax structure doesn't allow saving for a rainy day. (Mary Gregory)

4. *That grantmakers remain upbeat*

We want to be flexible. We want to help. We want to learn. (Larry Kressley)

There is the opportunity today to reconfigure, to reinvest, and to stay positive. (Ruby Lerner)

There is an amazing resiliency to the nonprofit and grantmaking sectors. (John E. Marshall, III)

Our foundation is not going away. We will continue to work with and support the nonprofit sector. (David Palenchar)

It is our job to help nonprofits succeed. (Karen Rosa)

Nonprofit organizations are well-meaning and well-intentioned. What a wonderful thing to be able to give people like that the money to try to change the world. There is a joy and magic to this business! (Bruce Esterline)

Appendix A

Sample Proposal

<date>
<name>
<title>
<fdn>
<address>
<City>

Dear <name>:

I am writing to request <fdn>'s support for historic King Manor Museum's new permanent exhibition, *Unearthing the Past: Archaeology at King Manor*. A grant of <amt> from <fdn> will enable King Manor Museum to present this innovative exhibition to our many visiting school groups and families.

Unearthing the Past tells the story of archaeology at King Manor, noting the results of several separate excavations and displaying artifacts found at the site. The exhibition's text reinforces the message of King Manor's Archaeology Education Program for schoolchildren: "It's not what you find, but what you find out." Presented in the North Kitchen, a space itself recently reinterpreted through archaeological data, the exhibition teaches basic concepts of archaeology and offers a lively glimpse into the lives of those who lived and worked at King Manor. *Unearthing the Past* has been carefully crafted to reinforce the themes of our popular archaeology education programs for 4th-6th grade students. Besides supporting our school outreach, the exhibition will inform and engage visiting adults and children.

The only historic house museum in southeast Queens, King Manor serves a largely minority and immigrant community and engages its audiences through historic site tours, interactive exhibits, lectures, public programs and school and community outreach. *Unearthing the Past* is a continuation of our efforts to use our significant archaeological collection to provide participatory learning experiences. To a population largely unfamiliar with the details of early American history, objects, such as those discussed and displayed in this exhibition, often speak louder than words.

We hope that <fdn> will help King Manor Museum offer *Unearthing the Past* to our many visitors. Thank you for your thoughtful consideration of this request.

Sincerely,

Mary Anne Mrozinski
Executive Director

A Proposal for Funding
Unearthing the Past: Archaeology at King Manor
To the <fdn>

Mary Anne Mrozinski
Executive Director
King Manor Association of Long Island, Inc.
90-04 161st St., Suite 704
Jamaica, New York 11432
Tel 718.206.0545
Fax 718.206.0541
E-mail Address: Kingmanor1@earthlink.net

Unearthing the Past: Archaeology at King Manor
TABLE OF CONTENTS

Proposal Summary

King Manor Museum, located in Jamaica, Queens, is the former home of distinguished American patriot and statesman Rufus King and three generations of his family. With significant collections of 18th- and 19th-century artifacts, archaeological finds and objects of historical significance, King Manor is a rich community resource in an area with few other connections to early American history. Through historic site tours, interactive exhibits, lectures, public programs and school and community outreach, we engage local residents and visitors in discovering early American history through the lives of those who lived and worked at King Manor.

We have recently completed planning and designing *Unearthing the Past: Archaeology at King Manor* and anticipate mounting this new permanent exhibition in 2004. It will lead viewers in an exploration of local history as members of the King household experienced it. As they investigate, visitors are encouraged to ask questions and think critically about the material presented. Artifacts found at the site illustrate our presentation of daily life in early Jamaica, supplemented by photographs, drawings, maps, and excerpts from historical documents. Through this exhibition, viewers will learn about fundamental archaeological concepts and steps in the process of archaeology and will come to understand history as an ongoing process.

Unearthing the Past will be an integral part of our Archaeology Education Program for 4th–6th grade students. In addition, the exhibition will serve our after-school and weekend visitors and will also be a resource for the children participating in our summer camp program. Because it reveals not only the process of archaeology but also the kinds of knowledge gleaned from careful excavation, this exhibition makes history more accessible to viewers. We hope the <fdn> will partner with King Manor Museum in making *Understanding the Past* available to our visitors.

Statement of Need

King Manor is the only historical resource serving southeast Queens, a racially and ethnically diverse community of 600,000. A large percentage of King Manor's audience is "non-traditional" as most visitors do not attend cultural events on a regular basis and many have never been to a museum. King Manor fills a need in our community for accessible, high quality educational and cultural activities that offer children, adults and families exposure to early American history and the issues that helped shape our nation.

Population Served

Every year, King Manor receives thousands of schoolchildren and many visitors from the local minority and immigrant communities. Our attendance has increased in recent years, from 4,370 visitors in 1995 to an average of over 8,000 in 2001 and 2002.

According to the 2000 census, Queens County is the most diverse in the nation. In our immediate service area (Jamaica and surrounding neighborhoods) more than 75% of residents are African American. Many residents are recent immigrants from the Caribbean, Africa, Central and South America, Eastern Europe, Korea and China. A higher percentage of Jamaica's residents receive public assistance than in the county as a whole. Our audience reflects this diversity.

Currently, the primary audiences for our school programs are the students, parents and teachers at NYC-metro area public and private schools, and the primary audiences for our public programs are adults (working and/or residing in Jamaica) and families. We expect attendance to reach 20,000-25,000 in the next five years through our continued community outreach and with the opening of the Jamaica Performing Arts Center and a Family Court facility, both across the street. With the completion of AirTrain to JFK Airport, local planners are projecting that travelers and tourists will increasingly visit Jamaica's downtown area.

Unearthing the Past: Archaeology at King Manor

In accordance with King Manor's mission, we strive to make history relevant and immediate to our audience. Through our programs and exhibitions, we foster in our visitors an understanding of the roots of the present and a deeper appreciation of history as an ongoing process. Stressing the fact that history is all around us, including beneath our feet, *Unearthing the Past* will help make history and its study more accessible and interesting to our diverse audience.

King Manor seeks to preserve and interpret the lives of those who lived and worked on the 122-acre farm—Rufus King, his family, and household and farm workers—and also everyday life in the community of Jamaica as microcosms of American history. This exhibition will introduce the study of artifacts as a means of learning about the past. In an area serving a largely minority and immigrant community, objects can often speak louder than words.

We will mount *Unearthing the Past* using artifacts uncovered at our site, images from excavations, objects from our collection, graphics of intact objects and excerpts from historic documents. The exhibition will show viewers how archaeology informs our knowledge and understanding of history—how we know what we know about the past. The processes prior to, during, and after archeological excavation are equally important in understanding an artifact and its story. Steps and concepts from the process of archaeology, such as research, stratigraphy, excavation techniques, recording data, and preservation ethics, will be discussed in text panels and illustrated with drawings, site photographs and objects.

Unearthing the Past will be installed in King Manor's North Kitchen, a room originally used for cooking and now welcoming school groups. The exhibit has been designed to maintain the multipurpose nature of this space, allowing us to continue to accommodate workshops and group programs. This particular room has seen extensive archaeology during recent capital projects; the findings of one excavation caused us to change the room's name (it was formerly known as the "Summer Kitchen") after food remains found in the room were consistent with winter usage. We also discovered that the room originally had a dirt floor and a rubble stone foundation and that a fire and subsequent rebuilding altered its original shape. These findings about the space now occupied by the exhibit are related in text and graphics throughout the exhibition and help bring archaeology to life for viewers.

We have designed several interactive features to complement the text and objects in the exhibition. One called "What's an Artifact?" involves visitors in determining which of several objects depicted on durable flashcards are actually artifacts. The text panel defines an artifact as "anything made by, changed by or used by humans," and viewers identify objects matching that description. The reverse of each card contains an answer and explanation. Near a set of panels discussing food remains is a display case with several animal bones, allowing visitors to use the graphics to match each bone to a historical cut of meat. They will also compare ceramic sherds found at King Manor to historical vessels to identify the kind of object from which the fragments originally came. These activities encourage critical thinking and invite viewers to become archaeologists and historians themselves.

This exhibition relies on artifacts and objects from the museum's collection. King Manor's archaeological collection contains more than 4,000 catalogued artifacts dating from the 18th to 20th centuries and is supported by comprehensive reports detailing four programs of archaeological testing and excavation at our site. Objects include numerous ceramic and glass sherds, metal artifacts, a gambling counter, medicine bottles, preserves jars, shells, animal bones, seeds, and other food remains. The collection is a rich community resource, providing an unparalleled opportunity to enhance and expand thematic interpretation of our site and community. This will be the first time our archaeology artifacts have been exhibited to the public.

Unearthing the Past was designed through The Exhibition Alliance's Small Museum Assistance Cooperative Exhibition Planning and Design Program. King Manor was one of only three organizations in New York State chosen to participate in this program. We anticipate fabricating and mounting the exhibition in 2004. Once installed in the North Kitchen, it will supplement our popular archaeology and history education programs for school children. In addition, the exhibition will offer an introduction to King Manor's history and the basic concepts and steps of archaeology for the thousands of adults and children we welcome every year.

Exhibition Goals

Through *Unearthing the Past*, we will challenge visitors to think about objects and how they relate to life in the past. In addition, the exhibition will enliven the stories of many members of the King household and the people of the village of Jamaica.

The exhibition will:

- Supplement and enhance our archaeology education programs, the only such resource for the school children of Queens;
- Emphasize the process of historical archaeology—the concepts, steps, and people involved—to support one of our primary program goals: "It's not what you find, but what you find out;"
- Challenge the public to think about objects and their relationship to history;
- Pose questions, whenever possible, rather than providing answers;
- Encourage viewers to ask their own questions of history;
- Reflect the highest possible interpretive and educational standards; and
- Incorporate current scholarship on historical archaeology at King Manor.

The exhibition's audience will:

- Experience the archaeological process through encountering questions, examining artifactual evidence, and drawing conclusions based on focused research materials; and
- Understand the ways in which archaeological discoveries could reveal aspects of daily life at King Manor through stories about the lives of its inhabitants.

Current Programs and Accomplishments

King Manor is a unique educational resource presenting public, school, and community outreach programs throughout the year.

- King Manor offers flexible **history education programs**—customized, thematic and seasonal—with age-appropriate activities designed to suit the needs of people with a wide variety of backgrounds. In 2001 and 2002, our education programs for public and private school students in the elementary grades through high school served an average of over 100 classes annually.

- Our local school district has joined with us to implement a newly-developed **Archaeology Education Program** for grades 4–6, for which New York State Council on the Arts has awarded planning and implementation grants. A pilot phase to introduce the program to school teachers and children began in 2001 with District 28 classes (including one class of special education mainstreamed children). We served 25 full classes by year-end 2002 and anticipate more in Spring 2003.

- **Public Programs and Special Events** are offered throughout the year and include community walking tours, lectures and slide presentations, behind-the-scenes tours of restoration work, concerts in the parlor and the Park, and demonstrations of historical crafts and chores. A wide variety of activities are designed to attract adults, children and families to King Manor and to involve them in learning more about the history of their community and the United States. Seasonal annual events such as Rufus' Egg Hunt, Historic Games Weekend and Christmas at King Manor have become community favorites and attract large numbers of visitors.

- Our new **Community Outreach Project** is promoting King Manor and its programs to civic, religious and service organizations and major employers in southeast Queens through a series of free group presentations and tours. The Project allows King Manor to tell its story and share its benefits with a new and potentially active audience.

- Once again this year we will partner with *The Constitution Works* to bring their innovative programs in teaching and interpreting the Constitution from Federal Hall in Manhattan to King Manor. With lesson plans and resources, teachers coach their students for several weeks, preparing them to assume the roles of justices, attorneys and senators. Students then argue a hypothetical case concerning the First Amendment and national security before the Supreme Court and debate an imaginary bill on the floor of the U.S. Senate. All this takes place within the historic setting of King Manor.

- Our **School-to-Career Internship Program** involves up to three part-time staff (2 Student Interns and 1 Seasonal Docent). The program provides opportunities for young people to explore career alternatives, develop practical skills and gain varied life and work experience as weekend interns.

2003 Initiatives

We are looking forward to the following new projects in 2003:

- Recent scholarship and analysis of our collection and King Manor reveal a much broader legacy and speak to increased relevance and greater potential for the museum. With a team of historians, educators, and consultants, we will develop a new **Interpretive Plan** to enhance and expand visitor experiences of this historic site.

- Our Curator, Nadezhda Williams, will oversee a **Cataloguing and Conservation Survey of the King Family Collection.** Nearly 100 items in number, this collection gives us valuable insight into individual members of the King family and the times in which they lived. From personal mementos to historically significant objects, this material will help us expand the museum's existing interpretation.

- Due to the great success of our archaeology and history education programs for 4th-6th grade students, we will offer an **Archaeology and History Summer Camp** for 9- to 12-year-olds in July 2003. The camp will expose fifteen to twenty interested students to archaeology at King Manor and the interaction between their own local history and the forces that shaped the United States. Evaluation of this pilot program will help us refine the camp for future years, when it will be presented in conjunction with Hofstra University's Archaeology Field School at our site.

History and Mission

King Manor Museum's mission is to involve and educate children and adults in local and national history through an innovative presentation of historic King Manor and its collection in the context of life in Jamaica, Queens and the United States in the early 19th century.

King Manor was the home of Rufus King (1755-1827), a distinguished figure in this nation's early history. King was a delegate to the Constitutional Convention in 1787, where he played an important role in forging the U.S. Constitution. As the first representative from New York elected to the United States Senate, King served three terms. Presidents George Washington, John Adams, Thomas Jefferson, and John Quincy Adams appointed him U.S. Ambassador to Great Britain. In 1816, King became the last candidate to run on the Federalist Party ticket for President of the United Sates, losing to James Monroe. Throughout his political career, Rufus King maintained an active anti-slavery stance and is known for his powerful speeches on the floor of the Senate opposing the Missouri Compromise.

In 1900, four years after the death of the last King family member in residence, King Manor Association of L.I., Inc. formed to preserve and care for King Manor. For more than one hundred years, KMA has sponsored educational programs while gathering an important collection of 18th and 19th century furniture, decorative arts, and memorabilia. King Manor is one of the finest examples of an early 19th century manor house in the New York City region.

Key Staff

King Manor has low overhead costs with only three paid full-time staff. All full-time staff devote substantial time to programs. King Manor's Executive Director Mary Anne Mrozinski has over 30 years of professional experience in the fields of art administration and education. Our Director of Education, Interpretation and Visitor Services, Kathleen Forrestal, has extensive historic house experience. David Gary is our Museum Education Assistant and Weekend Site Manager. In addition, our new part-time Curator (and former Director of Education) Nadezhda Williams joins us to care for King Manor's collections. Throughout the year over 20 volunteers assist with public programs, special events and in the gift shop.

Sustainability

King Manor Museum has received an initial $15,000 grant from The Bodman Foundation to begin work on *Unearthing the Past*. In addition to seeking both foundation and corporate support for the exhibition, we plan to apply for funding from the New York State Council on the Arts, the New York Council for the Humanities and the New York City Department of Cultural Affairs. The efforts of King Manor's Board members in seeking support from the local business community, within which several Board members are very active, will augment our grantseeking strategy.

Relationships with Other Jamaica Organizations

Regarded as one of the "flagships" of the Historic House Trust of New York City, King Manor works closely with Trust staff in program development and museum management. King Manor is one of twenty-two historic houses located on New York City-owned park land. The Department of Parks and Recreation, which owns the buildings, is responsible for the maintenance and restoration of their exteriors, while private groups are licensed to run the museums and care for the interiors.

Over the past decade, King Manor Association has enjoyed a particularly close working relationship with the Greater Jamaica Development Corporation, whose activities are centered on the economic revitalization of downtown Jamaica. King Manor is also one of the four founding members of Cultural Collaborative Jamaica (CCJ), with the Greater Jamaica Development Corporation, York College, and Jamaica Center for Arts and Learning. CCJ provides an effective and efficient way to market and increase audience development efforts for the group, which has grown to 14 members.

Evaluation

Evaluation of King Manor's programs, exhibitions and activities is ongoing. In 2000, King Manor completed an institutional assessment. In 2003, King Manor began an interpretive planning process through which historians, staff and consultants examine the site's potential and relevance in light of recent scholarship, evaluate the presentation of the collections and recommend strategies to increase our audience and engage them in exploring the past.

We will continue to track attendance by event/activity to monitor audience growth and diversity by age and other factors. Anecdotal feedback from visitors will be combined with our educators' informal assessment of what students learn as they explore the exhibition. King Manor works closely with local teachers to develop and assess programs; their formal assessments will guide changes to the exhibition.

Conclusion

Designed to introduce visitors to the process of archaeology and its findings at King Manor, *Unearthing the Past* will engage children and adults alike in a critical exploration of local history. Through the lens of King Manor's archaeological collection and historical documents, visitors will see how the King family, their household and farm employees and the residents of the Village of Jamaica lived in other centuries. Viewers will discover that finding an artifact is only the beginning of archaeology's discoveries, and that we may find out a great deal about daily life in the past through careful archaeology. We invite <fdn> to partner with King Manor Museum in presenting *Unearthing the Past* to our diverse audience.

King Manor Museum
Unearthing the Past: Archaeology at King Manor
Project Budget

Staff Salaries

Director of Interpretation, Education & Visitor Services (15% salary/fringe)	$ 6,375
Part-Time Curator (65% salary)	6,760
Executive Director (10% salary/fringe)	7,125
Total Staff Salaries	**$20,260**

Consulting Fees

Archaeologist (5 days @ $400)	$ 2,000
Total Consulting Fees	**$ 2,000**

Fabrication and Installation

Graphics	$ 8,800
Cases	22,770
Models	5,500
Mounts	1,760
Delivery	1,050
Installation	5,000
Lighting	5,000
Total Fabrication and Installation	**$49,880**

Travel, Lodging, Per Diem

Flights to Syracuse, NY (5 @ $175)	$ 875
Car rental/gas (2 @ $100)	200
Lodging (5 @ $125)	625
Per diem (5 @ $50)	250
Other local transportation costs	50
Total Travel, Lodging, Per Diem	**$ 2,000**

Other

Publicity	$4,000
Repair and recover floor; paint	6,000
Object preparation/conservation	2,000
Maintenance and custodial services	750
Insurance	1,500
Telephone	400
Photocopying	250
Total Other	$14,900

Total Exhibition Budget	**$89,040**

Appendix B

Selected Resources on Proposal Development

Compiled by Sarah Collins,
Manager of Bibliographic Services
The Foundation Center

Anderson, Cynthia. *Write Grants, Get Money.* Worthington, OH: Linworth Publishing, 2001.

> This is a proposal writing guidebook for school media specialists and other K–12 librarians who wish to improve library programs and facilities. Written for novice as well as veteran proposal writers, the book covers all stages of the proposal writing process. Appendix includes samples and a glossary.

Barbato, Joseph and Danielle S. Furlich. *Writing for a Good Cause: The Complete Guide to Crafting Proposals and Other Persuasive Pieces for Nonprofits.* New York, NY: Simon & Schuster, 2000.

> The authors share practical instructions about the art and craft of writing related to fundraising proposals, as well as case statements, newsletters, and other communications devices used by a typical development office. Includes glossary.

Barber, Daniel M. *Finding Funding: The Comprehensive Guide to Grant Writing*. 2nd ed. Long Beach, CA: Bond Street Publishers, 2002.
> This handbook provides advice for writers of proposals to government agencies, foundations, and corporations. The book includes a section on responding to a request for proposals and instructions for creating a letter proposal. Includes glossary.

Brewer, Ernest W., Charles M. Achilles, Jay R. Fuhriman, and Connie Hollingsworth. *Finding Funding: Grantwriting From Start to Finish, Including Project Management and Internet Use*. 4th ed. Thousand Oaks, CA: Corwin Press, 2001.
> The book is targeted to the education field and specifically to those submitting proposals to agencies of the federal government. Part 1 explores the research process and how to use the *Catalog of Federal Domestic Assistance* and other resources. Part 2 covers the elements of a standard proposal to a government agency or foundation, a sample proposal (funded by the U.S. Department of Education), and a discussion of how proposals are handled once received by funders. Part 3 relates to project management, explaining how to execute a project once it is funded.

Burke, Jim and Carol Ann Prater. *I'll Grant You That: A Step-by-Step Guide to Finding Funds, Designing Winning Projects, and Writing Powerful Grant Proposals*. Portsmouth, NH: Heinemann, 2000.
> The main part of the book is organized according to the sections of a proposal and covers project planning as well as proposal development. The book also explains how to write a letter of inquiry. Each chapter concludes with a checklist. The appendices contain a glossary and sample proposals.

Burke, Mary Ann. *Simplified Grantwriting*. Thousand Oaks, CA: Corwin Press, Inc., 2002.
> Directed primarily to schools and educators, the book offers templates and worksheets for planning programs, managing fund development work, and crafting proposals that succeed with grantmakers. With bibliographic references and an index.

Carlson, Mim. *Winning Grants Step by Step: The Complete Workbook for Planning, Developing and Writing Successful Proposals.* 2nd ed. San Francisco, CA: Jossey-Bass Publishers, 2002.

>This workbook contains instructions and exercises designed to help with proposal planning and writing and to meet the requirements of both government agencies and private funders. Provides a special resource section that includes how to research funders, how to evaluate a proposal through the funder's eyes, and a bibliography.

Clarke, Cheryl A. *Storytelling for Grantseekers: The Guide to Creative Nonprofit Fundraising.* San Francisco, CA: Jossey-Bass Publishers, 2001.

>Clarke puts forward the notion that proposals share much with great stories: characters, setting, and plot. She shows proposal writers how to craft documents that include elements of drama. The book also covers the research process and cultivation. Includes a sample letter of inquiry and sample budgets, as well as information on packaging the proposal.

Collins, Sarah, ed. *The Foundation Center's Guide to Winning Proposals.* New York, NY: The Foundation Center, 2003.

>The book reprints in their original form 20 proposals and four letters of inquiry that succeeded in securing foundation support. Each proposal is accompanied by commentary by the funder who awarded the grant and proposal writing advice. Includes glossary and bibliographical references.

Geever, Jane C., Liliana Castro Trujillo (trans.), and Marco A. Mojica (trans.). *Guía para escribir propuestas.* New York, NY: The Foundation Center, 2003.

>Prior third edition of this guide in Spanish. Includes new appendix of technical assistance providers who will assist Hispanic nonprofits.

Hall, Mary Stewart and Susan Howlett. *Getting Funded: The Complete Guide to Writing Grant Proposals.* 4th ed. Portland, OR: Portland State University, 2003.
> Hall explains the components of a standard proposal, with advice about project development and researching funders. This edition includes a recommended syllabus for those who teach proposal writing.

Karsh, Ellen and Arlen Sue Fox. *The Only Grant-Writing Book You'll Ever Need.* New York, NY: Carroll & Graf, 2003.
> Organized into a series of lessons, the book provides guidance to both nonprofits and individuals who are preparing proposals for public and private funders. Includes glossary.

Knowles, Cynthia. *The First-Time Grantwriter's Guide to Success.* Thousand Oaks, CA: Corwin Press Inc., 2002.
> This toolkit covers the elements of the proposal package, writing style, budget development, and other aspects of completing the application for grants from government and private sources. Includes glossary and bibliographic resources.

Kosztolanyi, Istvan. *Proposal Writing.* Baltimore, MD: Johns Hopkins University Institute for Policy Studies, 1997.
> This short book outlines the standard elements of a grantseeking proposal and includes a handy checklist. The pamphlet was specifically developed for nonprofit managers in Central and Eastern Europe and is available in Bulgarian, Czech, English, Hungarian, Polish, Russian, Slovak, and Slovene language editions.

Miller, Patrick W. *Grant Writing: Strategies for Developing Winning Proposals*, 2nd ed. Munster, IN: Patrick W. Miller and Associates, 2003.

> This manual for creating proposals to the federal government, specifically in response to requests for proposals (RFPs), begins with the activities that should precede the RFP and continues through post-submission efforts. Accompanied by numerous worksheets, charts, exercises, and exhibits, it provides suggestions for the narrative as well as the financial aspects of the proposal. Includes glossary.

New, Cheryl Carter and James Aaron Quick. *How to Write a Grant Proposal*. Hoboken, NJ: John Wiley & Sons, 2003.

> The authors cover the key elements of standard proposal formats, including the executive summary, need statement, project description, evaluation, and budget. Each chapter contains examples and checklists.

Nugent, Carol and Tom Ezell. *The Grantwriter's Start-Up Kit: A Beginner's Guide to Grant Proposals*. San Francisco, CA: Jossey-Bass Publishers, 2000.

> This 30-minute videotape discusses the basic elements of grant proposals and is accompanied by a workbook.

Orlich, Donald C. *Designing Successful Grant Proposals*. Alexandria, VA: Association for Supervision and Curriculum Development, 1996.

> The author presents the standard elements of proposal writing, with checklists at the end of each section. Includes a copy of a funded proposal and a reading list.

Quick, James Aaron and Cheryl Carter New. *Grant Seeker's Budget Toolkit*. Hoboken, NJ: John Wiley & Sons, 2001.

>   In this guidebook on project budgets, the authors explain the calculation of direct costs, with chapters specifically describing personnel and travel costs. The book also discusses the estimation of overhead and indirect costs and elaborates on the entire budgeting process, including writing the budget narrative. Sample budget worksheets are included.

Robinson, Andy. *Grassroots Grants: An Activist's Guide to Proposal Writing*. Berkeley, CA: Chardon Press, 1997.

>   The writer provides step-by-step guidance on how to create successful proposals, design projects, and manage grants. Four sample proposals are included.

APPENDIX C

Resources of the Foundation Center

The Foundation Center is a national service organization founded and supported by foundations to provide a single authoritative source of information on foundation and corporate giving. The Center's programs are designed to help grantseekers select those funders which may be most interested in their projects from the more than 76,000 active U.S. grantmakers. Among its primary activities toward this end are offering searchable databases online and on CD-ROM as well as publishing print directories covering foundation and corporate philanthropy; disseminating information on grantmaking, grantseeking, and related subjects through its site on the Internet; offering educational courses and workshops; and maintaining a nationwide network of library/learning centers and cooperating collections.

Databases and publications of the Foundation Center are the primary working tools of every serious grantseeker. They are also used by grantmakers, scholars, journalists, and legislators—in short, by anyone seeking any type of factual information on philanthropy. All private foundations and a significant number of corporate grantmakers actively engaged in grantmaking, regardless of size or geographic location, are included in one or more of the Center's databases or publications.

For those who wish to access information on grantmakers and their grants electronically, *The Foundation Directory Online Basic* provides information on 10,000 of the nation's largest foundations. *The Foundation Directory Online Plus* contains the top 10,000 foundations plus a searchable database of more than 350,000 grants. *The Foundation Directory Online Premium* includes 20,000 foundations plus over 350,000 grants. *The Foundation Directory Online Platinum* includes over 76,000 grantmakers plus over 350,000 grants.

The Center also issues *FC Search: The Foundation Center's Database on CD-ROM* containing the full universe of over 76,000 grantmakers and more than 320,000 associated grants.

Foundation Center print publications are of three kinds: directories that describe specific funders, characterizing their program interests and providing fiscal and personnel data; grants indexes that list and classify by subject recent foundation and corporate awards; and guides, monographs, and bibliographies that introduce the reader to funding research, elements of proposal writing, and nonprofit management issues.

In addition, the Center's award-winning Web site features a wide array of free information about the philanthropic community.

The Foundation Center's electronic and print products may be ordered from the Foundation Center, 79 Fifth Avenue, New York, NY 10003-3076, or online at our Web site. For more information about any aspect of the Center's programs or for the name of the Center's library collection nearest you, call 1-800-424-9836, or visit us on the Web at www.fdncenter.org. Please visit our Web site for the most current information available on new products and services of the Foundation Center.

ONLINE DATABASES

THE FOUNDATION DIRECTORY ONLINE SUBSCRIPTION PLANS

The Foundation Directory Online Basic

Search for foundation funding prospects from among the nation's largest 10,000 foundations and search the index of over 64,000 names of trustees, offices, and donors. Perform searches using up to twelve search fields and print results that appear in the browser window.
Monthly subscriptions start at $19.95 per month
Annual subscriptions start at $195 per year

The Foundation Directory Online Plus

Plus service allows users to search the 10,000 largest foundations in the U.S. and the index of over 64,000 names of trustees, offices, and donors—plus over 350,000 grants awarded by major foundations.
Monthly subscriptions start at $29.95 per month
Annual subscriptions start at $295 per year

The Foundation Directory Online Premium

Research and identify more foundation funding sources online with *The Foundation Directory Online Premium.* In addition to featuring 20,000 of the nation's large and mid-sized foundations and an index of over 111,000 names of trustees, officers, and donors—*Premium* service includes a searchable database of over 350,000 grants awarded by major U.S. foundations.
Monthly subscriptions start at $59.95 per month
Annual subscriptions start at $595 per year

The Foundation Directory Online Platinum

Search our entire universe of U.S. foundations, corporate giving programs, and grantmaking public charities—76,000+ funders in all—in our most comprehensive online subscription service. In addition to more funders, you'll get access to more in-depth data and an index of over 338,000 names of trustees, officers, and donors. Only *The Foundation Directory Online Platinum* offers extensive program details for 1,500+ leading foundations; detailed application guidelines for 7,200+ foundations; and sponsoring company information for corporate givers. This service also includes a searchable file of over 350,000 grants awarded by the largest U.S. foundations.
Monthly subscriptions start at $149.95
Annual subscriptions start at $995
Foundation and grants data are updated every two weeks for the above databases. Monthly, annual, multi-user, and institution wide access subscription options are available.
Please visit www.fconline to subscribe.

Foundation Grants to Individuals Online

Foundation Grants to Individuals Online features more than 6,000 foundation funding sources for individual grantseekers in education, research, arts and culture, or for special needs. Updated quarterly, users may choose from up to nine different search fields to discover prospective funders. Foundation records include current, authoritative data on the funder, including the name, address, and contact information; fields of interest; types of support; application information; and descriptions of funding opportunities for individual grantseekers.

One-month subscription: $9.95
Three-month subscription: $26.95
Annual subscription: $99.95

DIALOG

The Center's grantmaker and grants databases are also available online through The Dialog Corporation. For further information, contact The Dialog Corporation at 1-800-334-2564.

DIALOG User Manual and Thesaurus, Revised Edition

The *User Manual and Thesaurus* is a comprehensive guide that will help you retrieve essential fundraising facts quickly and easily. It will greatly facilitate your foundation and corporate giving research through our databases, offered online through Dialog.

November 1995 / ISBN 0-87954-595-X / $50

CD-ROMs

FC SEARCH: The Foundation Center's Database on CD-ROM, Version 8.0

The Foundation Center's comprehensive database of grantmakers and their associated grants can be accessed in this fully searchable CD-ROM format. *FC Search* contains the Center's entire universe of 76,000+ grantmaker records, including all known active foundations and corporate giving programs in the United States. It also includes over 320,000 newly reported grants from the largest foundations and the names of more than 338,000 trustees, officers, and donors which can be quickly linked to their foundation affiliations. Users can also link from *FC Search* to the Web sites of 4,000+ grantmakers and 2,200+ corporations.

Grantseekers and other researchers may select multiple criteria and create customized prospect lists which can be printed or saved. Basic or Advanced search modes and special search options enable users to make searches as broad or as specific as required. Up to 21 different criteria may be selected:

- grantmaker name
- grantmaker type
- grantmaker city
- grantmaker state
- geographic focus
- fields of interest
- types of support
- total assets
- total giving
- trustees, officers, and donors
- establishment date

- corporate name
- corporate location
- recipient name
- recipient city
- recipient state
- recipient type
- subject
- grant amount
- year grant authorized
- text search field

FC Search is a sophisticated fundraising research tool, but it is also user-friendly. It has been developed with both the novice and experienced researcher in mind. Assistance is available through Online Help, a *User Manual* that accompanies *FC Search,* as well as through a free User Hotline.

FC Search, Version 8.0, March 2004 (prices include fall 2004 Update disk plus one User Manual).
Standalone (single user) version: $1,195
Local Area Network (2–8 users in one building) version: $1,895*
Additional copies of User Manual: $19.95
New editions of FC Search are released each spring.
Larger local area network versions, site licenses, and wide area network versions are also available. For more information, call the **Electronic Product Support Line (Mon–Fri., 9 am–5 pm EST) 1-800-478-4661.*

THE FOUNDATION DIRECTORY 1 & 2 ON CD-ROM, Version 4.0

We've combined the authoritative data found in our two print classics, *The Foundation Directory* and *The Foundation Directory Part 2,* to bring you 20,000 of the nation's largest and mid-sized foundations in this searchable CD-ROM. Search for funding prospects by choosing from 12 search fields:

- grantmaker name
- grantmaker state
- grantmaker city
- fields of interest
- types of support
- trustees, officers, and donors

- geographic focus
- grantmaker type
- total giving
- total assets
- establishment date

The CD-ROM includes links to close to 1,300 foundation Web sites, a list of sample grants in over 10,500 foundation records, and a searchable index of over 111,000 trustees, officers, and donors.

The Foundation Directory 1 & 2 on CD-ROM
(includes March 2004 release and Fall 2004 Update disk)
Standalone (single-user) version: $495
Local Area Network version (2-8 users in one building): $795

THE FOUNDATION GRANTS INDEX ON CD-ROM, Version 4.0

The same data found in our classic print publication, *The Foundation Grants Index,* is available for the first time in a fast-speed CD-ROM format. Search our database of close to 125,000 recently awarded grants by the largest 1,000 funders to help you target foundations by the grants they have already awarded. Choose from twelve search fields:

- Recipient Name
- Recipient State
- Recipient City
- Recipient Type
- Grantmaker Name
- Grantmaker State
- Geographic Focus
- Subject
- Types of Support
- Grant Amount
- Year Authorized
- Text Search

The Foundation Grants Index on CD-ROM
December 2003/ Single User / ISBN 1-931923-74-4 /$165
Call 1-800-478-4661 for network versions.

GUIDE TO GREATER WASHINGTON D.C. GRANTMAKERS ON CD-ROM, Version 3.0

Compiled with the assistance of Washington Grantmakers, an organization with a unique local perspective on the dynamics of D.C. grantmaking, this CD-ROM covers more than 2,500 grantmakers located in the D.C. region or that have an interest in D.C.-area nonprofits. It also contains close to 3,000 selected grants and a searchable index of 8,000+ trustees, officers, and donors and their grantmaker affiliations.

Users can generate prospect lists within seconds, using twelve search fields. Grantmaker portraits feature crucial information: address, phone number, contact name, financial data, giving limitations, and names of key officials. For the large foundations—those that give at least $50,000 in grants per year—the volume provides even more data, including application procedures and giving interest statements.

The CD-ROM links to more than 150 grantmaker Web sites; connects to a special Web page with resources of value to D.C. grantseekers; and offers flexible printing and saving options and the ability to mark records.
June 2004 / Single-user: 1-931923-97-3 / $75
Local Area Network:* 1-931923-06-X / $125
*A local area network is defined as 2-8 users within one building.

GUIDE TO OHIO GRANTMAKERS ON CD-ROM

This new windows-compatible CD-ROM features profiles of over 3,400 foundations in Ohio, plus more than 400 funders outside the state that award grants in Ohio. This comprehensive searchable database provides current information on the foundations, corporate givers and public charities that make grants to Ohio-based nonprofits: crucial contact information,

financial data, names of key officials, and in many cases, application proce-
dures, giving interest statements, and a list of recent grants. *Guide to Ohio
Grantmakers on CD-ROM* is produced in collaboration with the Ohio
Grantmakers Forum and the Ohio Association of Nonprofit Organizations.
November 2003 / ISBN 1-931923-64-7 / $125

SYSTEM CONFIGURATIONS FOR CD-ROM PRODUCTS

- Windows-based PC
- Microsoft Windows^{TM} ME, Windows^{TM} 98, Windows^{TM}95,
  Windows^{TM}2000 or Windows^{TM}NT
- Windows^{TM}XP
- Pentium microprocessor
- 64MB memory

***Internet access and Netscape's Navigator or Communicator or Microsoft's Internet
Explorer browser required to access grantmaker Web sites and Foundation Center Web site.*

GENERAL RESEARCH DIRECTORIES

THE FOUNDATION DIRECTORY, 2004 Edition

The Foundation Directory has been widely known and respected in the field for
more than 40 years. It includes the latest information on the 10,000 largest U.S.
foundations based on total giving. The 2004 Edition includes over 1,500 foundations that are new to this edition. *Directory* foundations hold more than
$434 billion in assets and award over $24 billion in grants annually.

Each *Directory* entry contains information on application procedures, giving limitations, types of support awarded, the publications of each foundation, and foundation staff. In addition, each entry features such vital data
as the grantmaker's giving interests, financial data, grant amounts, address,
and telephone number. This edition includes over 39,000 selected grants. The
Foundation Center works closely with foundations to ensure the accuracy and
timeliness of the information provided.

The *Directory* includes indexes by foundation name; subject areas of interest; names of donors, officers, and trustees; geographic location; international interests; types of support awarded; and grantmakers new to the volume. Also included are analyses of the foundation community by
geography, asset and grant size, and the different foundation types.

Also available on CD-ROM and Online.
See sections on CD-ROMs and Online Databases.
March 2004
ISBN 1-931923-87-6 / $215
Published annually

THE FOUNDATION DIRECTORY PART 2, 2004 Edition

Following in the tradition of *The Foundation Directory*, *The Foundation Directory Part 2* brings you the same thorough coverage for the next largest set of 10,000 foundations. It includes *Directory*-level information on mid-sized foundations, an important group of grantmakers responsible for millions of dollars in funding annually. Essential data on foundations is included along with more than 34,000 recently awarded foundation grants, providing an excellent overview of the foundations' giving interests. Quick access to foundation entries is facilitated by seven indexes, including foundation name; subject areas of interest; names of donors, officers, and trustees; geographic location; international interests; types of support awarded; and grantmakers new to the volume.
March 2004 / ISBN 1-931923-88-4 / $185
Published annually

THE FOUNDATION DIRECTORY SUPPLEMENT

The Foundation Directory Supplement provides the latest-breaking information on *Foundation Directory* and *Foundation Directory Part 2* grantmakers six months after those volumes are published. Each year, thousands of policy and staff changes occur at these foundations. Fundraisers need to know about these crucial changes as rapidly as possible, as they may affect the way fundraisers prepare their grant proposals. The *Supplement* ensures that users of the *Directory* and *Directory Part 2* always have the latest addresses, contact names, policy statements, application guidelines, and financial data for the foundations they're approaching for funding.
September 2004 / ISBN 1-931923-89-2 / $125
Published annually

GUIDE TO U.S. FOUNDATIONS, THEIR TRUSTEES, OFFICERS, AND DONORS

This powerful fundraising reference tool provides fundraisers with current, accurate information on over 70,000+ private and community foundations in the U.S. The three-volume set also includes a master list of the names of the people who establish, oversee, and manage those institutions. With access to this information, fundraisers can facilitate their funding research by discovering the philanthropic connections of current donors, board members, volunteers, and prominent families in their geographic area. Because it provides a comprehensive list of U.S. foundations and the people who govern them, the *Guide to U.S. Foundations* also helps fundraisers follow up on any giving leads they may uncover. Each entry includes asset and giving amounts as well as geographic limitations, allowing fundraisers to quickly determine whether or not to pursue a particular grant source.

The *Guide to U.S. Foundations* is the only source of published data on thousands of local foundations. (It includes more than 50,000 grantmakers not covered in other print publications.) Each entry also tells you whether you can find more extensive information on the grantmaker in another Foundation Center reference work.

April 2004/ 1-931923-91-4 / $325
Published annually

THE FOUNDATION 1000

Nonprofit fundraisers and other researchers have access to annually published, comprehensive reports on the 1,000 largest foundations in the country. *The Foundation 1000* provides access to extensive and accurate information on this set of powerful funders. *Foundation 1000* grantmakers hold over $290 billion in assets and awarded close to 290,000 grants worth nearly $17 billion to nonprofit organizations nationwide.

The Foundation 1000 provides the most thorough analyses available of the 1,000 largest foundations and their extensive grant programs, including all the data fundraisers need most when applying for grants from these top-level foundations. Each multi-page foundation profile features a full foundation portrait, a detailed breakdown of the foundation's grant programs, and extensive lists of recently awarded foundation grants.

Five indexes give fundraisers the opportunity to target potential funders in a variety of ways: by subject field, type of support, geographic location, international giving, and the names of foundation officers, donors, and trustees.

October 2003 / ISBN 1-931923-60-4 / $295
Published annually

NATIONAL DIRECTORY OF CORPORATE GIVING, 9th Edition

Each year, corporations donate billions of dollars to nonprofit organizations. To help fundraisers tap into this vital source of funding, the *National Directory of Corporate Giving* offers authoritative information on over 3,600 company-sponsored foundations and direct corporate giving programs.

Fundraisers who want access to current, accurate fundraising facts on corporate philanthropies will benefit from the full range of data in this volume. The *National Directory of Corporate Giving* features detailed portraits of over 2,300 company-sponsored foundations plus over 1,300 direct corporate giving programs. Fundraisers will find essential information on these corporate grantmakers, including application information, key personnel, types of support generally awarded, giving limitations, financial data, and purpose and activities statements. Also included in the 9th Edition are over 6,500 selected grants. These grants give you the best indication of a grantmaker's funding priorities by identifying nonprofits it has already funded. The volume also provides data on the companies that sponsor foundations and direct-giving programs—essential background information for corporate grant searches. Each entry gives the company's name and address, a listing of its types of business, its financial data (complete with

Forbes and Fortune ratings), a listing of its subsidiaries, divisions, plants, and offices, and a charitable-giving statement.

The *National Directory of Corporate Giving* also features an extensive bibliography to guide you to further research on corporate funding. Seven essential indexes help you target funding prospects by geographic region; international giving; types of support; subject area; officers, donors, and trustees; types of business; and the names of the corporation, its foundation, and its direct-giving program.

August 2003/ ISBN 1-931923-59-0 / $195
Published annually

DIRECTORY OF MISSOURI GRANTMAKERS, 5th Edition

The *Directory of Missouri Grantmakers* provides a comprehensive guide to grantmakers in the state or that have an interest in Missouri nonprofits— over 2,300 foundations, corporate giving programs, and public charities— from the largest grantmakers to local family foundations. The volume will facilitate your grantseeking with information-filled entries that list giving amounts, fields of interest, purpose statements, selected grants, and much more. Indexes help you target the most appropriate funders by subject interest, types of support, and names of key personnel.

June 2003 / ISBN 1-931923-46-9 / $75
Published biennially

FOUNDATION GRANTS TO INDIVIDUALS, 13th Edition

The only publication devoted entirely to foundation grant opportunities for qualified individual applicants, the 13th Edition of this volume features more than 5,500 entries, all of which profile foundation grants to individuals. Entries include foundation addresses and telephone numbers, financial data, giving limitations, and application guidelines. This volume will save individual grantseekers countless hours of research.

June 2003 / ISBN 1-931923-45-0 / $65
Published biennially

SUBJECT DIRECTORIES

The Foundation Center's National Guide to Funding series is designed to facilitate grantseeking within specific fields of nonprofit activity. Each of the directories described below performs the crucial first step of fundraising research by identifying a set of grantmakers that have already stated or demonstrated an interest in a particular field. Fact-filled entries provide access to foundation addresses, financial data, giving priorities, application procedures, contact names, and key officials. Many entries also feature recently awarded grants, the best indication of a grantmaker's funding priorities. A variety of indexes help fundraisers target potential grant sources by subject area, geographic preferences, types of support, and the names of donors, officers, and trustees.

Subject guides are published biennially.

GUIDE TO FUNDING FOR INTERNATIONAL AND FOREIGN PROGRAMS, 7th Edition

The *Guide to Funding for International and Foreign Programs* covers over 1,300 grantmakers interested in funding projects with an international focus, both within the U.S. and abroad. Program areas covered include international relief, disaster assistance, human rights, civil liberties, community development, education, and much more. The volume also includes descriptions of more than 8,900+ recently awarded grants.
May 2004 / ISBN 1-931923-95-7 / $125

NATIONAL GUIDE TO FUNDING IN AIDS, 3rd Edition

This volume covers more than 560 foundations, corporate giving programs, and public charities that support AIDS- and HIV-related nonprofit organizations involved in direct relief, medical research, legal aid, preventative education, and other programs to empower persons with AIDS and AIDS-related diseases. Over 500 recently awarded grants show the types of projects funded by grantmakers.
June 2003/ ISBN 1-931923-44-2 / $115

NATIONAL GUIDE TO FUNDING IN ARTS AND CULTURE, 8th Edition

This volume covers more than 7,500 grantmakers with an interest in funding dance companies, museums, theaters, and countless other types of arts and culture projects and institutions. The volume also includes more than 16,500 descriptions of recently awarded grants.
May 2004 / ISBN 1-931923-94-9 / $155

NATIONAL GUIDE TO FUNDING FOR THE ENVIRONMENT AND ANIMAL WELFARE, 7th Edition

This guide covers over 2,900 grantmakers that fund nonprofits involved in international conservation, ecological research, waste reduction, animal welfare, and much more. The volume includes descriptions of over 7,200 recently awarded grants.
June 2004 / ISBN 1-931923-93-0 / $125

NATIONAL GUIDE TO FUNDING IN HEALTH, 8th Edition

The *National Guide to Funding in Health* contains essential facts on nearly 10,700 grantmakers interested in funding hospitals, universities, research institutes, community-based agencies, national health associations, and a broad range of other health-related programs and services. The volume also includes descriptions of more than 16,000 recently awarded grants.
May 2003 / ISBN 1-931923-42-6 / $155

NATIONAL GUIDE TO FUNDING FOR LIBRARIES AND INFORMATION SERVICES, 7th Edition

This volume provides essential data on more than 800 grantmakers that support a wide range of organizations and initiatives, from the smallest public

libraries to major research institutions, academic/research libraries, art, law, and medical libraries, and other specialized information centers. The volume also includes descriptions of over 600 recently awarded grants.
May 2003 / ISBN 1-931923-43-4 / $115

NATIONAL GUIDE TO FUNDING IN RELIGION, 7th Edition

With this volume, fundraisers who work for nonprofits affiliated with religious organizations have access to information on nearly 8,400 grantmakers that have demonstrated or stated an interest in funding churches, missionary societies, religious welfare and education programs, and many other types of projects and institutions. The volume also includes descriptions of more than 10,000 recently awarded grants.
May 2003/ ISBN 1-931923-41-8 / $155

GRANT DIRECTORIES

GRANT GUIDES

Designed for fundraisers who work within defined fields of nonprofit development, this series of guides lists actual foundation grants of $10,000 or more in 12 key areas of grantmaking.

Each title in the series affords immediate access to the names, addresses, and giving limitations of the foundations listed. The grant descriptions provide fundraisers with the grant recipient's name and location; the amount of the grant; the date the grant was authorized; and a description of the grant's intended use.

In addition, each *Grant Guide* includes three indexes, which help fundraisers target possible sources of funding by the type of organization generally funded by the grantmaker, the subject focus of the foundation's grants, and the geographic area in which the foundation has already funded projects.

Each *Grant Guide* also includes a concise overview of the foundation spending patterns within the specified field. The introduction uses a series of statistical tables to document such important findings as (1) the 25 top funders in your area of interest (by total dollar amount of grants); (2) the 15 largest grants reported; (3) the total dollar amount and number of grants awarded for specific types of support, recipient organization type, and population group; and (4) the total grant dollars received in each U.S. state and many foreign countries.

The *Grant Guide* series gives fundraisers the data they need to target foundations making grants in their field, to network with organizations that share their goals, and to tailor their grant applications to the specific concerns of grantmakers as expressed by the grants they have already made.
Series published annually in December / 2003 / 2004 Editions / $75 each

GUIDEBOOKS, MANUALS, AND REPORTS

ARTS FUNDING IV: An Update on Foundation Trends

This report provides a framework for understanding trends in foundation funding for arts and culture through 2001. Based on a sample of 800+ foundations, it compares growth in arts funding with other sources of public and private support, examines changes in giving for specific arts disciplines, analyzes giving patterns by region, and explores shifts in the types of support funders award. Prepared in cooperation with Grantmakers in the Arts.
July 2003 / ISBN 1-931923-48-5 / $19.95

FAMILY FOUNDATIONS: A Profile of Funders and Trends

Family Foundations is an essential resource for anyone interested in understanding the fastest growing segment of foundation philanthropy. The report provides the most comprehensive measurement to date of the size and scope of the U.S. family foundation community. Through the use of objective and subjective criteria, the report identifies the number of family foundations and their distribution by region and state, size, geographic focus, and decade of establishment; and includes analyses of staffing and public reporting by these funders. *Family Foundations* also examines trends in giving by a sample of larger family foundations between 1993 and 1998 and compares these patterns with independent foundations overall. Prepared in cooperation with the National Center for Family Philanthropy.
August 2000 / ISBN 0-87954-917-3 / $19.95

INTERNATIONAL GRANTMAKING II:
An Update on U.S. Foundation Trends, 2nd Edition

An update to 1997's groundbreaking *International Grantmaking* study, this report documents trends in international giving by U.S. foundations in the late 1990s. Based on a sample of over 570 foundations, *International Grantmaking II* identifies shifts in international giving priorities, types of support provided, recipients funded, and countries/regions targeted for support. The report also includes an overview of recent events and factors shaping the international funding environment; and perspectives on the changing funding climate based on a 2000 survey of more than 25 leading international grantmakers. Prepared in cooperation with the Council on Foundations.
November 2000 / ISBN 0-87954-916-5 / $35

THE FOUNDATION CENTER'S GRANTS CLASSIFICATION SYSTEM
INDEXING MANUAL WITH THESAURUS, Revised Edition

A complete "how-to" guide, the *Grants Classification Manual* provides an essential resource for any organization that wants to classify foundation grants or their recipients. The *Manual* includes a complete set of all classification codes to facilitate precise tracking of grants and recipients by subject, recipient type, and population categories. It also features a completely revised thesaurus to help identify the "official" terms and codes that represent

thousands of subject areas and recipient types in the Center's system of grants classification.
May 1995 / ISBN 0-87954-644-1 / $95

FOUNDATIONS TODAY SERIES, 2004 Edition

The *Foundations Today Series* provides the latest information on foundation growth and trends in foundation giving. Individual copies may be ordered separately or together at a special savings.

Foundation Giving Trends: Update on Funding Priorities—*Examines 2003 grantmaking patterns of a sample of more than 1,000 larger U.S. foundations and compares current giving priorities with trends since 1980.*
February 2004/ISBN 1-931923-71-X/$45

Foundation Growth and Giving Estimates: 2003 Preview—Provides a first look at estimates of foundation giving for 2003 and final statistics on actual giving and assets for 2002. Presents new top 100 foundation lists.
April 2004/ISBN 1-931923-72-8/$20

Foundation Yearbook: Facts and Figures on Private and Community Foundations—Documents the growth in number, giving, and assets of all active U.S. foundations from 1975 through 2002. *June 2004/ISBN 1-931923-96-5/$45*
Three Book Set / ISBN 1-931923-96-5 / $95

THE FOUNDATION CENTER'S GUIDE TO GRANTSEEKING ON THE WEB, 2003 Edition

Learn how to maximize use of the Web for your funding research. Packed with a wealth of information, the *Guide to Grantseeking on the Web* provides both novice and experienced Web users with a gateway to the numerous online resources available to grantseekers. Foundation Center staff experts have team-authored this guide, contributing their extensive knowledge of Web content as well as their tips and strategies on how to evaluate and use Web-based funding materials. Presented in a concise, "how-to" style, the *Guide* will introduce you to the Web and structure your funding research with a toolkit of resources. These resources include foundation and corporate Web sites, searchable databases for grantseeking, government funding sources, online journals, and interactive services on the Web for grantseekers.
September 2003 / Book / ISBN 1-931923-67-1 / $29.95
CD-ROM / ISBN 1-931923-73-6 / $29.95
Book and CD-ROM / $49.95

GUÍA PARA ESCRIBIR PROPUESTAS

The Spanish language translation of the *Guide to Proposal Writing*, 3rd edition includes a special appendix listing consultants and technical assistance providers who can help Spanish speakers craft proposals in English, or give advice on fundraising.
March 2003 / ISBN 1-931923-16-7 / $34.95

THE FOUNDATION CENTER'S GUIDE TO WINNING PROPOSALS

The *Guide to Winning Proposals* features twenty grant proposals that have been funded by some of today's most influential grantmakers. Each proposal—reprinted in its entirety—includes a critique by the program officer, executive director, or other funding decision-maker who granted the proposal. The accompanying commentary points to the strengths and weaknesses of each proposal and provides insights into what makes some proposals more successful than others.

To represent the diversity of nonprofits throughout the country, proposals have been selected from large and small, local and national organizations, and for many different support purposes, including basic budgetary support, special projects, construction, staff positions, and more. The *Guide to Winning Proposals* also includes actual letters of inquiry, budgets, cover letters, and vital supplementary documents needed to develop a complete proposal.

October 2003 / ISBN 1-931923-66-3 / $34.95

NEW YORK METROPOLITAN AREA FOUNDATIONS:
A Profile of the Grantmaking Community

This study examines the size, scope, and giving patterns of foundations based in the eight-county New York metropolitan area. It documents the New York area's share of all U.S. foundations; details the growth of area foundations through 2000; profiles area foundations by type, size, and geographic focus; compares broad giving trends of New York area and all U.S. foundations between 1992 and 2000; and examines giving by non-New York area grantmakers to recipients in the New York area. Prepared in cooperation with the New York Regional Association of Grantmakers.

December 2002 / ISBN 1-931923-52-3/ $24.95

THE PRI DIRECTORY: Charitable Loans and Other Program-Related Investments by Foundations, 2nd Edition

Certain foundations have developed an alternative financing approach—known as program-related investing—for supplying capital to the nonprofit sector. PRIs have been used to support community revitalization, low-income housing, microenterprise development, historic preservation, human services, and more. This directory lists leading PRI providers and includes tips on how to seek out and manage PRIs. Foundation listings include funder name and state; recipient name, city, and state (or country); and a description of the project funded. There are several helpful indexes to guide PRI-seekers to records by foundation/recipient location, subject/type of support, and recipient name, as well as an index to officers, donors, and trustees.

September 2003/ ISBN 1-931923-49-3 / $75

SOUTHEASTERN FOUNDATIONS II: A Profile of the Region's Grantmaking Community, 2nd Edition

Southeastern Foundations II provides a detailed examination of foundation philanthropy in the booming 12-state Southeast region. The report includes an overview of the Southeast's share of all U.S. foundations, measures the growth of Southeastern foundations since 1992, profiles Southeastern funders by type, size, and geographic focus, compares broad giving trends of Southeastern and all U.S. foundations in 1992 and 1997, and details giving by non-Southeastern grantmakers to recipients in the region. Produced in cooperation with the Southeastern Council of Foundations.
November 1999 / ISBN 0-87954-775-8 / $19.95

OTHER PUBLICATIONS

AMERICA'S NONPROFIT SECTOR: A Primer, 2nd Edition
by Lester M. Salamon

In this revised edition of his classic book, Lester M. Salamon clarifies the basic structure and role of the nonprofit sector in the U.S. Moreover, he places the nonprofit sector into context in relation to the government and business sectors. He also shows how the position of the nonprofit sector has changed over time, both generally and in the major fields in which the sector is active. Illustrated with numerous charts and tables, Salamon's book is an easy-to-understand primer for government officials, journalists, and students—in short, for anyone who wants to comprehend the makeup of America's nonprofit sector.
February 1999 / ISBN 0-87954-801-0 / $14.95

BEST PRACTICES OF EFFECTIVE NONPROFIT ORGANIZATIONS: A Practitioner's Guide
by Philip Bernstein

This volume provides guidance for any nonprofit professional eager to advance your organization's goals. Philip Bernstein has drawn on his own extensive experience as a nonprofit executive, consultant, and volunteer to produce this review of "best practices" adopted by successful nonprofit organizations. The author identifies and explains the procedures which provide the foundation for social achievement in all nonprofit fields. Topics include defining purposes and goals, creating comprehensive financing plans, evaluating services, and effective communication.
February 1997 / ISBN 0-87954-755-3 / $29.95

THE BOARD MEMBER'S BOOK: Making a Difference in Voluntary Organizations, 3rd Edition

by Brian O'Connell

The revised and expanded edition of this popular title by former Independent Sector President, Brian O'Connell, is the perfect guide to the issue, challenges, and possibilities that emerge from the interchange between a nonprofit organization and its board. O'Connell offers practical advice on how to be a more effective board member as well as on how board members can help their organizations make a difference.
March 2003 / ISBN 1-931923-17-5 / $29.95

INVESTING IN CAPACITY BUILDING: A Guide To High-impact Approaches

by Barbara Blumenthal

This new publication by Barbara Blumenthal offers guidance to grantmakers and consultants in designing better approaches to helping nonprofits, while showing nonprofit managers how to obtain more effective assistance. Grantmakers recognize that technical assistance grants and general support have had a modest impact overall in promoting stability, effectiveness, and efficiency in the nonprofits that they support. Based on interviews with over 100 grantmakers, intermediaries, and consultants; 30 evaluations of capacity building programs; and a review of research on capacity building; *Investing in Capacity Building: A Guide to High-Impact Approaches* identifies the most successful strategies for helping nonprofits improve organizational performance.
September 2003 / ISBN 1-931923-65-5 / $34.95

CAREERS FOR DREAMERS AND DOERS: A Guide to Management Careers in the Nonprofit Sector

by Lilly Cohen and Dennis R.Young

A comprehensive guide to management positions in the nonprofit world, *Careers for Dreamers and Doers* offers practical advice for starting a job search and suggests strategies used by successful managers throughout the voluntary sector.
November 1989 / ISBN 0-87954-294-2 / $29.95

ECONOMICS FOR NONPROFIT MANAGERS

by Dennis R. Young and Richard Steinberg

Economics for Nonprofit Managers is a complete course in the economic issues faced by America's nonprofit decision-makers. Young and Steinberg treat micro-economic analysis as an indispensable skill for nonprofit managers. They introduce and explain concepts such as opportunity cost, analysis at the margin, market equilibrium, market failure, and cost-benefit analysis. This volume also focuses on issues of particular concern to nonprofits, such as the economics of fundraising and volunteer recruiting, the regulatory environment, the impact of competition on nonprofit performance, interactions among sources of revenue, and much more.
July 1995 / ISBN 0-87954-610-7 / $34.95

EFFECTIVE ECONOMIC DECISION-MAKING BY NONPROFIT ORGANIZATIONS

by Dennis R. Young

Editor Dennis R. Young offers useful, practical guidelines to support today's nonprofit managers in their efforts to maximize the effectiveness with which their organizations employ their valuable resources. Nonprofit managers and leaders must advance their mission while balancing the agendas of trustees, funders, staff, and government. In this context, this group of expert authors explores core operating decisions that face all organizations and provides solutions that are unique to nonprofits of any size. Chapters cover such key decision-making areas as pricing of services, compensation of staff, outsourcing, fundraising expenditures, and investment and disbursement of funds. Published by the National Center on Nonprofit Enterprise and the Foundation Center

December 2003 / ISBN 1-931923-69-8 / $34.95

HANDBOOK ON PRIVATE FOUNDATIONS

by David F. Freeman and the Council on Foundations

This publication provides a thorough look at the issues facing the staff and boards of private foundations in the U.S. Author David F. Freeman offers sound advice on establishing, staffing, and governing foundations and provides insights into legal and tax guidelines as well. Each chapter concludes with a useful annotated bibliography. Sponsored by the Council on Foundations.

September 1991
Softbound: ISBN 0-87954-404-X / $29.95
Hardbound: ISBN 0-87954-403-1 / $39.95

THE NONPROFIT ENTREPRENEUR: Creating Ventures to Earn Income

Edited by Edward Skloot

In a well-organized topic-by-topic approach to nonprofit venturing, non-profit consultant and entrepreneur Edward Skloot demonstrates how nonprofits can launch successful earned-income enterprises without compromising their missions. Skloot has compiled a collection of writings by the nation's top practitioners and advisors in nonprofit enterprise. Topics covered include legal issues, marketing techniques, business planning, avoiding the pitfalls of venturing for smaller nonprofits, and a special section on museums and their retail operations.

September 1988 / ISBN 0-87954-239-X / $19.95

A NONPROFIT ORGANIZATION OPERATING MANUAL: Planning for Survival and Growth

by Arnold J. Olenick and Philip R. Olenick

This straightforward, all-inclusive desk manual for nonprofit executives covers all aspects of starting and managing a nonprofit. The authors discuss legal

problems, obtaining tax exemption, organizational planning and development, and board relations; operational, proposal, cash, and capital budgeting; marketing, grant proposals, fundraising, and for-profit ventures; computerization; and tax planning and compliance.
July 1991 / ISBN 0-87954-293-4 / $29.95

PEOPLE POWER: SERVICE, ADVOCACY, EMPOWERMENT
by Brian O'Connell

Throughout his career, Brian O'Connell has broadened the impact of his own nonprofit work with thoughtful essays, speeches, and op-ed articles. *People Power,* a selection of O'Connell's most powerful writings, provides thought-provoking commentary on the nonprofit world. The 25+ essays included in this volume range from keen analyses of the role of voluntarism in American life, to sound advice for nonprofit managers, to suggestions for developing and strengthening the nonprofit sector of the future. Anyone involved in the nonprofit world will appreciate O'Connell's penetrating insights.
October 1994 / ISBN 0-87954-563-1 / $24.95

PHILANTHROPY'S CHALLENGE
Building Nonprofit Capacity Through Venture Grantmaking
by Paul B. Firstenberg

In this new book, Paul Firstenberg challenges grantors to proactively assist grantee management as the way to maximize the social impact of nonprofit programs, while showing grantseekers how the growing grantor emphasis on organizational capacity building will impact their efforts to win support. The author draws on his years of experience working within both nonprofit and for-profit organizations to explore the roles of grantor and grantee within various models of venture grantmaking. To emphasize the importance that nonprofit boards can play in this process, a full chapter is devoted to governance issues and responsibilities.
January 2003
Softbound: ISBN 1-931923-15-9 / $29.95
Hardbound: ISBN 1-931923-53-1 / $39.95

PROMOTING ISSUES AND IDEAS: A Guide to Public Relations for Nonprofit Organizations, Revised edition
by M Booth & Associates

M Booth & Associates are specialists in promoting the issues and ideas of nonprofit groups. Their book presents proven strategies that will attract the interest of the people you wish to influence and inform. Included are the "nuts-and-bolts" of advertising, publicity, speech-making, lobbying, and special events; how to write and produce informational literature that leaps off the page; public relations on a shoe-string budget; how to plan and evaluate PR efforts; the use of rapidly evolving communication technologies; and a new chapter on crisis management.
December 1995 / ISBN 0-87954-594-1 / $29.95

RAISE MORE MONEY FOR YOUR NONPROFIT ORGANIZATION:
A Guide to Evaluating and Improving Your Fundraising
by Anne L. New

In *Raise More Money,* Anne New sets guidelines for a fundraising program that will benefit the incipient as well as the established nonprofit organization. The author divides her text into three sections: "The Basics," which delineates the necessary steps a nonprofit must take before launching a development campaign; "Fundraising Methods," which encourages organizational self-analysis and points the way to an effective program involving many sources of funding; and "Fundraising Resources," a 20-page bibliography that highlights the most useful research and funding directories available.
January 1991 / ISBN 0-87954-388-4 / $14.95

SECURING YOUR ORGANIZATION'S FUTURE:
A Complete Guide to Fundraising Strategies,
Revised Edition
by Michael Seltzer

In this completely updated edition, Michael Seltzer acts as your personal fundraising consultant. Beginners get bottom-line facts and easy-to-follow worksheets; veteran fundraisers receive a complete review of the basics plus new money-making ideas. Seltzer supplements his text with an extensive bibliography of selected readings and resource organizations. Highly recommended for use as a text in nonprofit management programs at colleges and universities.
February 2001 / ISBN 0-87954-900-9 / $34.95

SUCCEEDING WITH CONSULTANTS:
Self-Assessment for the Changing Nonprofit
by Barbara Kibbe and Fred Setterberg

This inspirational book, written by Barbara Kibbe and Fred Setterberg and supported by the David and Lucile Packard Foundation, guides nonprofits through the process of selecting and utilizing consultants to strengthen their organization's operations. The book emphasizes self assessment tools and covers six different areas in which a nonprofit organization might benefit from a consultant's advice: governance, planning, fund development, financial management, public relations and marketing, and quality assurance.
April 1992 / ISBN 0-87954-450-3 / $19.95

THE 21ST CENTURY NONPROFIT
by Paul B. Firstenberg

In *The 21st Century Nonprofit,* Paul B. Firstenberg provides nonprofit managers with the know-how to make their organizations effective agents of change. The 21st Century Nonprofit encourages managers to adopt strategies developed by the for-profit sector in recent years. These strategies will help them to expand their revenue base by diversifying grant sources,

exploit the possibilities of for-profit enterprises, develop human resources by learning how to attract and retain talented people, and explore the nature of leadership through short profiles of three nonprofit CEOs.
July 1996 / ISBN 0-87954-672-7 / $34.95

MEMBERSHIP PROGRAM

ASSOCIATES PROGRAM
A Special Membership Program

The Associates Program puts important facts and figures on your desk through e-mail access to our staff, helping you to:

- identify potential sources of foundation funding for your organization; and
- gather important information to use in targeting and presenting your proposals effectively.

Your annual membership in the Associates Program ($995) gives you vital information on a timely basis, saving you hundreds of hours of research time.

Take Advantage of These Services:

- Convenient e-mail access to our staff.
- Consultations with Foundation Center information specialists who can help you develop initial prospect lists of foundation funders.
- Free individual or small group training sessions to learn how to use any of our online database or CD-ROM products.
- Biographical information on trustees, officers, and prospective donors.
- Help finding research reports, books, and articles on any topic related to fundraising or nonprofit management.
- A document delivery option for the most recent foundation tax returns from our database of 990-PF forms and our extensive collection of grantmaker annual reports.

Free Subscription to Associates E-News Alert

Members can sign up for an e-mail service that provides lists of hundreds of new and emerging foundations each month as well as updates to the Foundation Center's grantmaker database.

Associates Program Online

Exclusive access to Associates Program Online, a members-only Web site that connects Associates to a variety of services and offers additional content not available to the general public, including up-to-the-minute notice of changes at foundations and a list of those that have terminated. "Associates on the Move" and "Spotlight On" features highlight professional activities of members and their organizations.

Additional Member Benefits

- Invitation to Associates-only briefings on critical issues and the opportunity to learn from experts and network with colleagues.
- A free *Grant Guide* of your choice (for new members only).
- A free subscription to the reports in the *Foundations Today Series* (for new members only).
- No prepayment required for Center books, training programs, and CD-ROMs.
- Discounts on seminar registration and other special offers throughout the year.

Put our staff of experts to work for your fundraising program. For more information call 1-800-424-9836, or visit our Web site at www.fdncenter.org.

FOUNDATION CENTER'S WEB SITE www.fdncenter.org

Helping grantseekers succeed, helping grantmakers make a difference

The Foundation Center's Web site (www. fdncenter.org) is the premier online source of fundraising information. Updated and expanded on a daily basis, the Center's site provides grantseekers, grantmakers, researchers, journalists, and the general public with easy access to a range of valuable resources, among them:

- Personalization at the Center's Web site allows registered users to receive content tailored to their fundraising and research interests at key areas of the site, including the home page, *Philanthropy News Digest,* and the Marketplace.
- A Grantmaker Web Sites area provides annotated links to more than 2,400 grantmaker sites that can be searched by subject or geographic key words.
- Foundation Finder, our free foundation look-up tool, includes foundation contact information and brief background data, such as type of foundation, assets, total giving, and EIN, as well as links to 990-PFs (IRS tax filings).
- *Philanthropy News Digest* features current philanthropy-related articles abstracted from major media outlets, interviews, original content, and the "PND Talk" message board. PND is also available as a weekly listserv.
- *The Literature of the Nonprofit Sector Online,* a searchable bibliographical database, includes 22,500+ entries of works on the field of philanthropy, over 14,000 of which are abstracted.

- Our Online Library features comprehensive answers to FAQs, an online librarian to field questions about grantseeking and the Foundation Center, annotated links to useful nonprofit resources, and an online orientation to the grantseeking process.

- Our popular Virtual Classroom allows visitors to link to a Proposal Writing Short Course (in English and Spanish); Establishing a Nonprofit Organization; Demystifying the 990-PF; and more.

- Information about Center-sponsored orientations, training programs, and seminars can be found on our Library home page and in the marketplace.

- The locations of our 200+ Cooperating Collections nationwide, and the activities and resources at our five main libraries.

- A "For Individual Grantseekers" area introduces individuals to the grantseeking process and provides tools and resources to help individuals get started.

- A special section, "For Grantmakers," offers funders the opportunity to help get the word out about their work, answers frequently asked questions, and informs grantmakers on recent developments in the field and how the Center assists grantees and applicants.

- The "For the Media" area provides journalists with current information on key developments in private philanthropy in the U.S.

- Sector Search is a search tool that continuously crawls the Web sites of thousands of private, corporate, community foundations, grantmaking public charities, and nonprofit organizations, and provides relevant, accurate search results. Search by organization type, subject, or individual's name.

All this and more is available at our Web site. The Center's publications and electronic resources can be ordered at the site's Marketplace. Visit our Web site often for information on new products and services.

About the Author

Jane C. Geever is chairman of the development consulting firm, J. C. Geever, Inc. The firm, founded by Ms. Geever in 1975, was the first woman-led fundraising company admitted into membership in the American Association of Fund Raising Counsel (AAFRC).

Among her achievements, she assisted in the creation of the certificate program in fund raising at New York University, spearheaded the first jobs bank at the National Society of Fund Raising Executives' (NSFRE)[*] International Conference and New York NSFRE's Fundraising Day, and was appointed to the Independent Sector's ad hoc committee on Values and Ethics. Ms. Geever is a member of the advisory council for the national project *Funding Fundraising* at Baruch College and is active in Independent Sector's *Give Five* program in New York. She has been a member of the board and officer of the NSFRE Institute and of the AAFRC.

---

[*] Now known as the Association of Fundraising Professionals.

Ms. Geever holds a Master's Degree from the New School for Social Research, and she has done post-graduate study in business management at Stanford University. She delivered the May 1989 commencement address at the 71st commencement of her alma mater, Seton Hill College in Greensburg, Pennsylvania, at which time she received an honorary Doctor of Humane Letters degree.

Ms. Geever is a nationally recognized author and lecturer. She teaches seminars in association with the Foundation Center on proposal writing and approaching foundations and corporate funders.